# Logo art

Innovation in Logo Design

Charlotte Rivers

A RotoVision Book

Published and distributed by RotoVision SA
Route Suisse 9
CH-1295 Mies
Switzerland

RotoVision SA
Sales and Editorial Office
Sheridan House, 114 Western Road
Hove BN3 1DD, UK
Tel: +44 (0)1273 72 72 68
Fax: +44 (0)1273 72 72 69
www.rotovision.com

Originally published in hardback 2008
This edition © RotoVision SA 2009

10 9 8 7 6 5 4 3 2 1
ISBN: 978-2-88893-104-1

Art Director: Jane Waterhouse
Design: Simon Slater, www.laki139.com

Reprographics in Singapore by ProVision Pte. Ltd.
Tel: +65 6334 7720   Fax: +65 6334 7721

Printed in China by Midas Printing International Ltd.

# Contents

01

"A logo has to introduce itself compellingly to the viewer in the tone and manner befitting the project or brand, whatever that may be."

**Adrian Clifford, Australia**

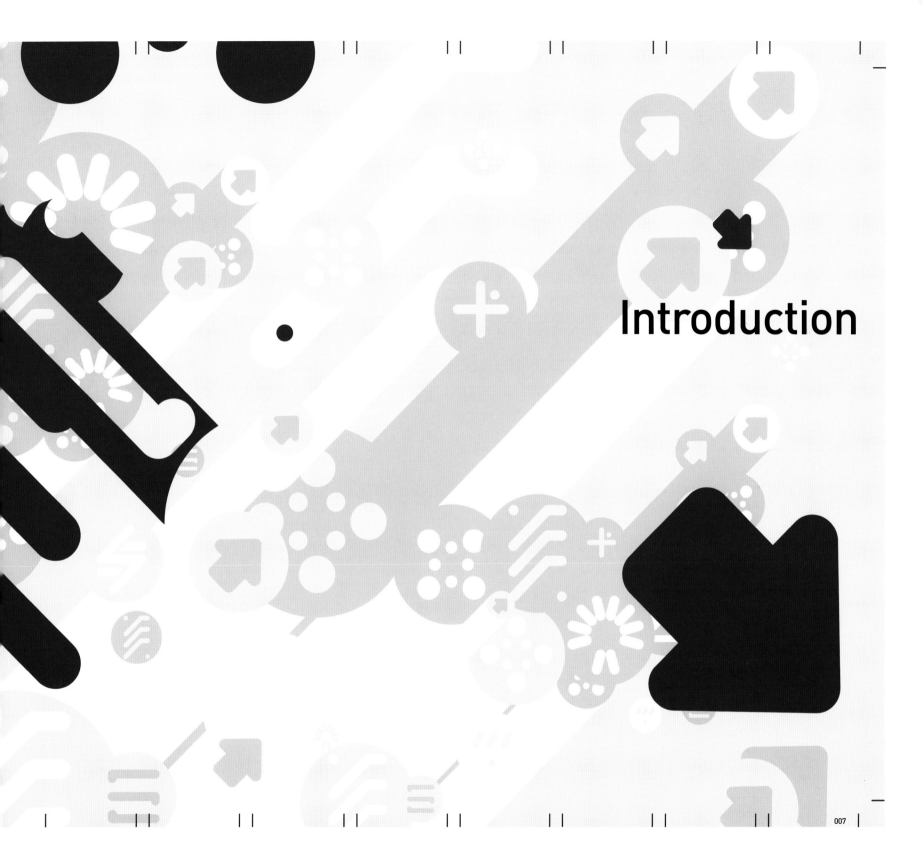

# Introduction

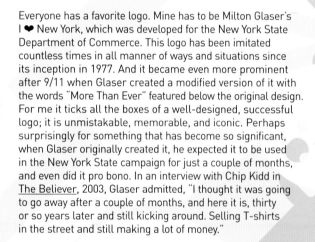

Everyone has a favorite logo. Mine has to be Milton Glaser's I ❤ New York, which was developed for the New York State Department of Commerce. This logo has been imitated countless times in all manner of ways and situations since its inception in 1977. And it became even more prominent after 9/11 when Glaser created a modified version of it with the words "More Than Ever" featured below the original design. For me it ticks all the boxes of a well-designed, successful logo; it is unmistakable, memorable, and iconic. Perhaps surprisingly for something that has become so significant, when Glaser originally created it, he expected it to be used in the New York State campaign for just a couple of months, and even did it pro bono. In an interview with Chip Kidd in The Believer, 2003, Glaser admitted, "I thought it was going to go away after a couple of months, and here it is, thirty or so years later and still kicking around. Selling T-shirts in the street and still making a lot of money."

Glaser's I ❤ New York has become a major part of popular culture and social language; it comes in a long line of other significant logos designed since the idea of corporate identity began at the end of the nineteenth century. Companies such as Coca-Cola, Campbell's Soup, Quaker Oats, and H. J. Heinz were some of the first to use brand names and branded packaging to sell their products, and Peter Behrens' identity design in 1907 for German electrical firm AEG is widely regarded as one of the first major corporate identity systems commissioned.

The trend for such identities continued to grow throughout the twentieth century and into the twenty-first. Some of the best-known global examples include Herb Lubalin's Families and Marriage logos, Paul Rand's work for ABC and IBM, Saul Bass's work for United Airlines and AT&T, and Walter Landor's FedEx logo. The 1970s saw logo design and corporate identities become big business. Companies and organizations around the world, small or large, felt the need for a logo to market and promote their products. These logos were used not only to identify a company and its products, but also to instill trust in a particular brand, and consumers bought into this.

Another significant moment in the history of logo design came in 1980 when Canada became the first nation to adopt a symbol and logotype. Today things are slightly different. "Not trusted" and "corporation" often appear in the same sentence; the subversion of logos in magazines such as Adbusters and in Naomi Klein's No Logo indicate that corporations and their large, expensive identities are no longer connecting with consumers as they used to. However, despite this, companies large and small still require logos. From entire nations to independent photographers, the logo is an important part of any company's communication.

Designing logos, or logotypes, is one of the primary jobs of any graphic designer. Many start by designing one for themselves. A logo is generally described as a graphic or typographical sign or symbol that represents a particular company or organization, product, or service. It becomes the cornerstone of a company image and forms the base of the wider visual identity—its corporate identity. A logo should be unique, functional, succinct, and representative of the company, organization, product, or service that it has been designed for. As Stefan Sagmeister says, "Sometimes a logo has to work as a unifier, putting all the various pieces of an organization together. Sometimes it needs to work as a mark of quality, telling a consumer that this has been made and approved by a certain entity. At other times there will be a need for a transformer, showing off the flexibility of a program." Or, as Adrian Clifford of Rinzen says, "A logo has to introduce itself compellingly to the viewer in the tone and manner befitting the project or brand, whatever that may be." Both good points highlight the need for a logo to communicate a company's values and philosophy to its target market.

There are five basic types of logo: text only (e.g. Coca-Cola and FedEx logos); image only (e.g. Nike's "swoosh," Apple Inc's apple, and The Red Cross' red cross); text and image (e.g. I ❤ New York and Adidas's triple-blade logos); abbreviation only (e.g. IBM's logo); and abbreviation and image (e.g. the BP logo). This book showcases a selection of all of these types of logos, only from less corporate companies than those mentioned in the above examples. The content of Logo-Art focuses on smaller, independent companies' logos from around the world. Their logos are no less considered or professionally designed; the only difference is that, in some cases, they tend to be more creative. Examples include logos created by designers for self-promotion (such as Chris Bilheimer's logo for his talk at the AIGA) together with those created for larger organizations (such as Roanne Adams' logo for the not-for-profit educational organization Wingspan Arts). The logos showcased here include those for the music industry, the world of fashion, media and events, charities and services, and design and the creative arts. And, from the USA to Malaysia to France and Australia, this book shows that there is some great logo design being produced in all corners of the world today. Enjoy!

**Charlotte Rivers**

# 02

"A good logo is like meeting an interesting person. I like logos that tell a story."

**Emmi Salonen, UK**

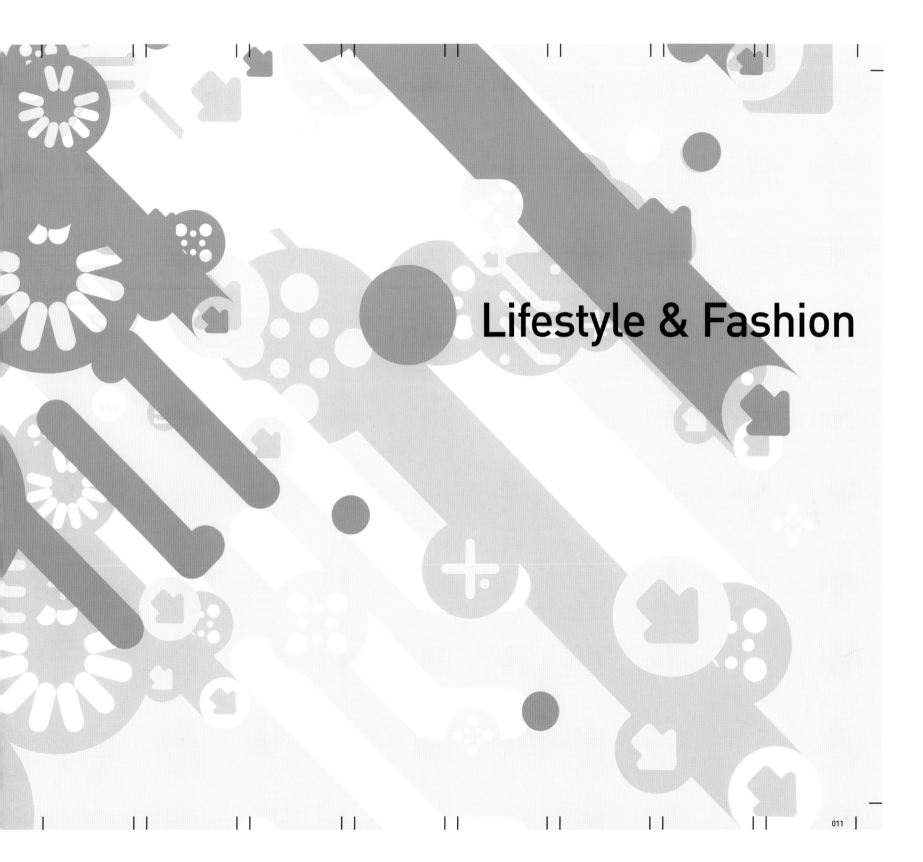

Lifestyle & Fashion

"A good logo is appropriate, distinctive, and timeless. It bears the weight of its identity conclusively and indivisibly."

**Adrian Clifford, Australia**

# Introduction

Designing logos for lifestyle and fashion brands differs from designing logos for other types of businesses in that often, the consumer buys into the brand as a whole. For instance, people buy clothes from certain fashion houses because of what surrounds it—the brand's advertising, the press coverage the label might achieve, the celebrities who wear that brand's clothes, and of course the "look" of the brand identity. Because of this, designing a logo for a fashion brand is not only about being its visual voice and representing it in the marketplace, but also about reflecting its potential consumers' taste and style. The following pages show some great examples of this, from snowboarding stores to London-based fashion brands as well as nonfashion examples such as toy stores and cafés.

Client: **Jonathan Morr Group**
Design: **Base Design**
Country: **USA**

## Stand

The Jonathan Morr Group specializes in developing high-end hotel and restaurant concepts around the world. Stand, one such venue, is a burger restaurant that references the "Americana" of burger joints and diners, but in a sophisticated way. Base Design was commissioned to create a logo for the restaurant. "The concept for the logo is based on the type and copy. The typeface, Berthold Block, has a slightly uneven contour and boldness that is beefy/meaty, and the stacked logo resembles a burger," explains Base Design. The logo has been applied throughout the restaurant and included on its stationery, packaging, buttons, matchbooks, and menus.

Client: **Lulu&Red**
Design: **Tom Lancaster at Stylo Design**
Country: **UK**

## Lulu&Red

Lulu&Red is a small fashion design company. Its logo needed to be "friendly and approachable" and to incorporate a cat, as the company was named after the two founders' cats. "We took our inspiration from this and with a simple addition to the ampersand, the cat problem was dealt with," explains Lancaster. An amended version of American Typewriter Bold was used for the logo lettering.

Client: **The Studio by ProWolfMaster**
Design: **milkxhake**
Country: **Hong Kong**

## The Studio
## by ProWolfMaster

The Studio by ProWolfMaster, a US street-fashion store, asked milkxhake to create a unique logotype for its launch in Hong Kong. milkxhake combined an Avant Garde typeface with an italic script-style typeface to generate a harmonic mixture of contemporary and fashionable graphic culture for the brand identity. The logotype was applied to all stationery items, and to hangtags and T-shirts. milkxhake also designed a promotional poster for the store, using funky objects to spell out the brand name. The poster was first printed in gold ink, with overprint black on textured paper, to generate a unique, fashionable appearance.

Client: **Lee Cooper**
Design: **Nigel Cabourn and
        Simon Glover at ODD**
Country: **UK**

## FU's

When fashion outlet UFO, owned by Steinberg, rejected the rights to sell Lee's collection, the founders of Lee reacted by creating FU's (**** You Steinberg) so they could sell the collection themselves. FU's thrived throughout the 1970s, representing antiestablishment and alternative values, before being bought by Lee Cooper. ODD was commissioned to redefine FU's identity to make it one of the world's elite denim brands. "We wanted to express all the history and emotion wrapped up in the original brand," explains Glover. "The final identity was inspired primarily by the visual language that surrounded FU's in its 1960s and 1970s heyday, and aims to capture this language and hark back to that era, but with a modern twist that makes it fit comfortably in today's graphic and brand landscape." The project was completed in partnership with Cabourn—globally renowned for his unique approach to denim, and to labeling systems.

Client: **Modern British Canteen Ltd.**
Design: **Luke Powell and Jody Hudson-Powell at Hudson-Powell**
Country: **UK**

## Canteen

"The concept behind the Canteen brand image was to create a wordmark, symbol, and graphic style that had longevity and that was in step with the democratic, contemporary aesthetic of the dining room and its food offering," explain Powell and Hudson-Powell. Canteen's Creative Director Clayton-Malone had the idea to use a shield as the Canteen mark as it was symbolic of the partnership between different parties that is central to the restaurant's philosophy. This idea was developed into the current symbol, a simplified traditional shield. This has been used together with an adapted version of Johnston Light typeface for the Canteen wordmark.

Client: **Question Air**
Art Direction: **Dan Witchell**
Design: **Proud Creative**
Country: **UK**

## Frequently Asked Questions

Question Air sells products from such designers as Vivienne Westwood, Paul Smith, and J. Lindeberg through its boutiques, and online exclusives from People of the Labyrinths, Trosman, Sharon Wauchob, Bodyamr, and DVB through its website. Frequently Asked Questions (FAQ) is a sub-brand and own label for Question Air. Proud Creative was commissioned to create a simple and memorable identity for FAQ. "We came up with a very simple typographic solution for the label," explains Witchell. "We used Avant Garde and Avant Garde Gothic for the logo, which was applied to clothing, labels, and in store."

Client: **kauzwear**
Design: **Tim Bollinger at Via Grafik**
Country: **Germany**

## pflanzen (flowers)

kauzwear, a small fashion label, commissioned Bollinger to design a logo for its 2005 summer collection. He used an unusual combination of images—electronic devices and flowers—to "create a surreal moment. This logo was inspired by nature and technology," he explains. "It is a combination of living things and dead things." The logo has been used on the brand's T-shirts and on its website.

Client: **Smått & Rått**
Design: **Christian Albriktsen**
Country: **Norway**

## oioi.no

Smått & Rått is a toy store specializing in radio-controlled cars, boats, and planes. When the store launched its website, the owners wanted a different, memorable domain name, hence oioi.no, Norwegian for "wow wow." Albriktsen explains, "I often find logos with domain names a little boring. To prevent this, I made the dot into a shooting star." He also slanted the logo, so it appears to be bouncing off the ground, reflecting the playfulness of the store. "I wanted the logo to represent the toys the store sells, so gave it a round, playful, bouncy feel." The logo is based on Cooper Black, modified by Albriktsen.

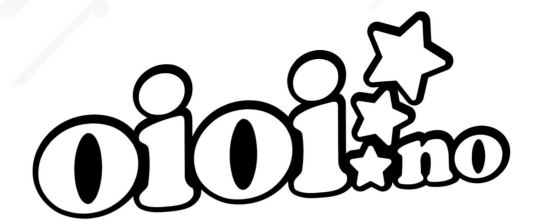

Client: **STUDIO at Fred Segal**
Design: **Dave Bravenec at**
**Braveland Design**
Country: **USA**

## STUDIO at Fred Segal

STUDIO is an independent store located in Fred Segal, a hip boutique that includes several upcoming clothing labels and product stores. It specializes in beauty supplies and hairstyling for men and women. "The client wanted us to create a modern-looking logo with a simple typeface that would represent all the cosmetic products in the store," explains Bravenec. The logo design is based on the American flag layout, with its blue block and red stripes, but instead of stars the word STUDIO appears in the top left corner. The typeface used was drawn by Bravenec. The logo has been applied to all print pieces and interior signage; it was even made into a clear adhesive seal for use on a white wall.

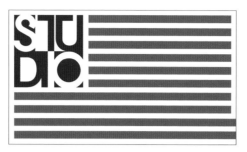

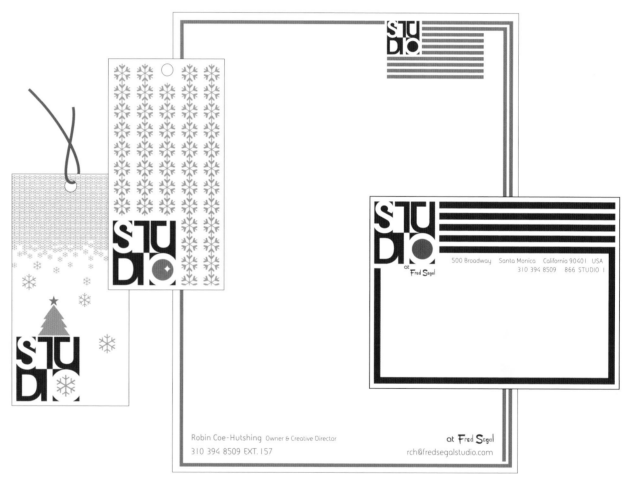

Client: **KYN**
Design: **Ariel Aguilera and Andrea Benyi**
    at **Pandarosa**
Country: **Australia**

## Kid You Not (KYN)

KYN wines commissioned Pandarosa to create a logo for its launch, using modern-day characters to tell its story. "As in many childhood stories, the wise characters we created—an Owl and a Fox—are intended to add a sense of mystery, darkness, and adventure to the KYN identity," explain Aguilera and Benyi. "We aimed to evoke a sense of nostalgia, while still maintaining a contemporary, yet classic aesthetic. By evoking memories and bringing them to a current base, we wanted to engage the audience in a dialogue about their own fables." The logo and characters appear on KYN's wine labels, packaging, and website.

Client: **Danny's Deli**
Design: **Emmi Salonen at Emmi**
Country: **UK**

## Danny's Deli

The brief for this sandwich shop's identity was to create something strong and fun that wasn't space-specific, because the owners intended to open more branches in the future. "I wanted to have some fun with the identity and so the chopped sandwich 'D' came about," explains Salonen. "It immediately shows not only what they do, but also the fast turnover of sandwiches during busy lunchtimes." Lubalin Gothic typeface was chosen for its uppercase D, which works well as a shape for the sandwich. The logomark works well independently on napkins, sugar sachets, cups, and bags.

Client: **On & Of**
Design: **Julio Dui at Grafikonstruct**
Country: **Brazil**

## On & Of

On & Of's brief to Dui was to create something that was expressive, yet simple—a logo that could be understood by anyone. "For a lighting-design company, what could be a more direct expression of its product than a lightbulb?" says Dui. "The lamp is a device for giving light, so I decided to use it for the logo, together with the company name, On & Of." Dui designed the rounded typeface used in the logo to contrast with the pixelated nature of the lightbulb image.

Client: **Livraria Boa Vista**
Design: **Julio Dui at Grafikonstruct**
Country: **Brazil**

## Livraria Boa Vista

The owner of this bookstore used to work on a coffee plantation called Boa Vista. Wanting a link between the two, he adopted that name for his store. Dui followed this thinking. "I wanted to use something in the logo that referenced both the farm and the bookstore," he explains. "The coffee plantation made me think of 'trees,' and of course books come from trees, so it seemed like a good symbol for the shop."

Client: **Sue Stemp**
Design: **Deanne Cheuk**
Country: **USA**

## Sue Stemp

Sue Stemp, a New York–based fashion designer, commissioned Cheuk to tweak an already existing logo to make it suitable for use on a variety of items. "Sue Stemp's clothes are very fun and feminine and she works with a lot of printed patterns. The logo redesign needed to be as interesting as the clothes," explains Cheuk. The result is a logo with Bodoni set over a montage of hand-drawn images. It has been applied across hangtags, packing tape, address labels, and Stemp's corporate stationery. The logo was laser-cut from paper for the hangtags, and laser-cut from metal for a specially produced box.

Client: **Emmetts Hair Salon**
Design: **Paul Reardon at Peter & Paul/Birdseed**
Country: **UK**

## Emmetts Hair Salon

Emmetts' brief stipulated that the logo be versatile enough to work on both large-scale applications like signage and window graphics, and small-scale applications like appointment cards. "We wanted to create something expressive and gestural to contrast with most of the hair products in salons," explains Reardon. The logo was hand-drawn, scanned, then redrawn to make it organic and free-flowing.

Client: **Six Wines Eight**
Design: **Tim Balaam at Hyperkit**
Country: **UK**

## Six Wines Eight

Six Wines Eight aims to simplify wine selection by grouping the wines it sells by style and representing each style with a particular color. Within each style wines are organized by price. Its brief to Hyperkit was to produce a logo to reflect its fresh approach to wine retailing, with elements that would suit different situations. "We established a vine-like grid from which we derived a bespoke typeface and logo," explains Balaam. "It was our intention that the logo had a life across many different formats, from stationery to promotional postcards, packaging, stickers, catalog, website, and signage for the store." The palette of colors was chosen so that each represents a different style of wine.

Client: **Emma Elliott**
Art Direction: **Dan Witchell**
Design: **Proud Creative**
Country: **UK**

## Dogmad

Emma Elliot is an entrepreneur with a love of dogs and fashion. She set up Dogmad to create interesting clothing for dog owners and stylish products for dogs. She commissioned Proud Creative to create a strong, quirky, memorable identity that would appeal to savvy dog owners, and work across a variety of materials. "The concept of the logo was to show very simple silhouettes of dogs blending with straightforward typography," explains Witchell. "So simple, quirky messages on T-shirts are designed to make an instant impact." The typeface used is VAG Rounded.

Client: **Work in Progress Distribution**
Design: **Mat Fowler at Playarea**
Country: **UK**

## The Three Threads

The Three Threads' name refers not only to the three principal partners (Carhartt, Edwin, and Pointer) of Work In Progress, the distribution company that owns it, but also to "Three Threads" beer, which was created right next to the store. Hence, the brief was for the store identity to hint toward pub and brewery imagery, but with its own modern take. In addition the store owners planned to launch their own clothing under the name, so the logo had to work across many applications, from large-scale store signage to small-scale garment embroideries. "The logo has been drawn up especially to control the weight and impact of the icon, so it can work on all levels of scale and application," explains Fowler. "The bronze and black color palette is to reflect and pay homage to beer labels and pub signs of old." The identity typeface is based on Avant Garde, with modifications to specific characters to play on the three Ts and Hs in the name, The Three Threads.

THE THREE THREADS®

THE THREE THREADS®  THE THREE THREADS®

# BRUNO GRIZZO

Client: **Bruno Grizzo**
Design: **Matthias Ernstberger**
Country: **USA**

## Bruno Grizzo

New York–based fashion designer Bruno Grizzo marked the launch of his collection in 2006 by winning two coveted Gen Art style awards. Grizzo's fashion is modern, yet classic, elegant, and understated. For the launch of his first collection, he commissioned Ernstberger to create a logo to reflect and communicate the essence of the brand. "The vision for the design was a contemporary, elegant face with a very unique character," explains Ernstberger. He used a custom-designed typeface for the logo, which was applied on stationery items, Grizzo's website, lookbooks, and in advertising.

Client: **The Grateful Palate**
Design: **Dave Bravenec at**
     **Braveland Design**
Country: **USA**

## SUXX

The Grateful Palate specializes in wine and product imports. Not happy with the initial concept of their own wine brand, The Grateful Palate gave Braveland Design full creative control, "but wanted the brand to read as a wine label and not just an isolated logo on the bottle," explains Bravenec. "They suggested certain treatments that might appeal to a younger demographic and not the traditional wine consumer." The logo's look comes from early bitmap typefaces, and the double XX has been used to give the brand a more modern, edgier feel. The back of the label lists items that people say SUXX in their daily lives, concluding with "WINE SUXX, SUXX SUXX." The typeface was drawn by Bravenec and the logo was applied on wine labels using embossing and screen glossing to give the surface effect of pixel formations.

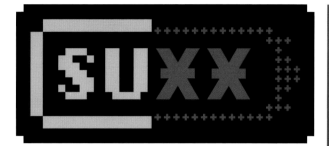

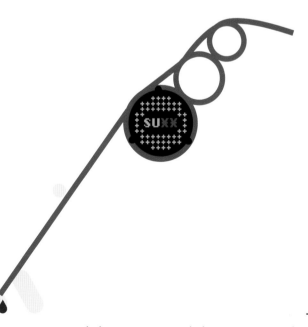

Client: **Elisabeth Arkhipoff**
Design: **Elisabeth Arkhipoff**
    at **Romantic Surf**
Country: **USA**

## Unexpected Feeling & Sons

This logo is part of Arkhipoff's ongoing personal project Unexpected Feeling & Sons, an arts-meets-fashion scheme that features a series of found objects customized by Arkhipoff, then released under her Unexpected label. There have been several collections to date, all of which were accompanied by a series of supporting graphics and sold via a website. Arkhipoff wanted to create a logo for the brand that was timeless and would work across the various items in the collection. She has reworked a version of Futura to create the logo.

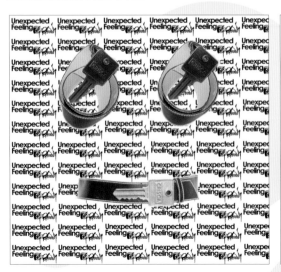

Client: **Granola**
Design: **Claus Due at Designbolaget**
Country: **Denmark**

## Granola

Granola, a coffee bar, "has the look of a Danish diner from the mid-1950s, and Sam Cooke playing on the stereo. This, together with the slightly rockabilly look of the owner, gave us a pretty good idea about where to go with the logo." Due has created a logo that is a modern version of a 1950s idea, using the typefaces DIN Mittelschrift and Clarendon. The logo has been used on street signs, windows, postcards, and giftwrap.

Client: **The 50-50 Company**
Design: **Christian Albriktsen**
Country: **Norway**

## 50-50 Sticker Sheet

50-50 is a 10-year-old skateboard and snowboard store; its owners also run Norway's biggest online store. "Kids involved in skateboarding are usually fanatical about stickers so all these 50-50 logos are part of a sticker sheet that is intended to be enclosed in every purchase online as well as in the stores," Albriktsen explains. "So, the brief was basically to design a bunch of logos for this sticker sheet which worked out great, as I've done lots of work for them over the years and have a pretty good idea of what they want and what they don't want." Albriktsen's ideas came mainly from the company's playfulness and what it's about, generally reflecting what goes on in the skateboarding scene.

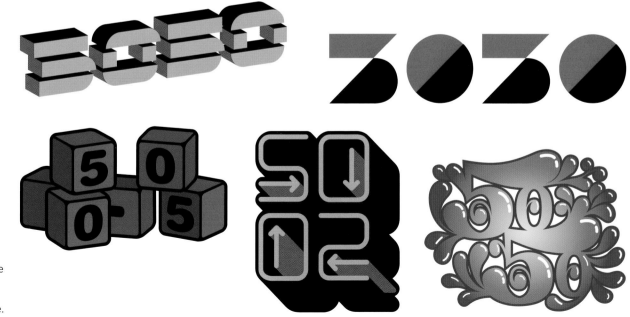

Client: **WoodWood (DK)**
Design: **Micke Thorsby at PMKFA**
Countries: **Japan/Germany**

## WoodWood

WoodWood is a Danish clothing store
and label with an outlet in Berlin. For the
logo Thorsby "wanted to use typography
as illustration and vice versa. I wanted
to visualize the way I built 3-D objects as
a kid, cutting and pasting, gluing letters
together, using Styrofoam and stuff."
He based his design on the Neographik
typeface, developing it in order to create
3-D lettering.

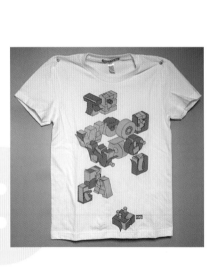

Client: **Rome SDS**
Design: **Christian Hundertmark
at C100 Studio**
Countries: **Germany/USA**

## Rome SDS

C100 Studio designed this logo for the
American snowboard company Rome
SDS; it was used as part of a snowboard's
graphics, which C100 also designed.
The brief was to create a graphic for
a women's free-ride board. "The idea
behind the design was punk meets high
fashion," explains Hundertmark. "We
then designed this logo around the board
graphics." The hand-drawn, decorative
logotype is also featured on a snowboard.

Client: **Isolée**
Design: **Alex Cañada at
Design People Studio**
Country: **Spain**

## Isolée

Isolée is a multimedia space that specializes in fashion, food, and lifestyle. Design People Studio designed this hand-drawn illustrative version of the actual company logo. It was then applied to Isolée workers' clothing using silkscreen printing. "Inspiration for the design came from the work of illustrated words Love & Hate by Maria Monferrer," explains Cañada, "as requested by the Isolée founder."

# FIVE EIGHT ZERO

# FIVE EIGHT ZERO

**JACKSON
RIGHT OLD TWO &
GROUND**

**ALIVE
MAIDS A'MILKING
TOLERANCE**

Client: **580 Ltd.**
Design: **Patrick Duffy at No Days Off**
Country: **UK**

## 580

580 is the parent company of three London bars—The Lock Tavern, Keston Lodge, and The Defector's Weld. Its brief for a new logo was that it be simple, cool, and fit in with the bars' philosophy of quality, style, and a sense of fun. "The concept is simple," explains Duffy. "We took the number 580 and wrote it out in Helvetica Neue 85 Heavy as words instead of numerals. We then added other words either onto the beginning or end, making new, humorous, surreal combinations." The concept reflects the bars' outlook while retaining a sober look and feel more in keeping with the business end of the operation.

Client: **Superyou**
Design: **Stefan Claudius**
Country: **Germany**

## Superyou

Superyou is a clothing brand run by
Michelle Wirtz, a friend of this logo's
designer, Stefan Claudius. "The brief
was open. The only condition was that it
be possible to screenprint the logo onto
T-shirts," explains Claudius. "The idea
was to create a logo out of the 'S' and 'Y'
of Superyou and to make it as abstract
as possible." Inspired by Asian, and in
particular Thai design, Claudius created
this abstract symbol for Wirtz: the logo
on the left is an earlier iteration of the
final logo, on the right. "I started with
a font that I designed, CA Emeralda,"
explains Claudius. "I then modified the
letterforms heavily in order to create
the letters that make up the logo."

Client: **Gorgeously Flawed**
Design: **Paul Sych at Faith**
Country: **Canada**

## Gorgeously Flawed

This wordmark was self-published by
Sych. "I just enjoyed the juxtaposition and
tension between these two words and the
extreme contrast that they share," he
explains. "There was no direct client, it
was just something that I wanted to do;
create something that looked gorgeous,
simple, ugly, and flawed all at the same
time, and to poke fun at the fashion
industry and what it stands for." For this
logo design, Sych found inspiration in
fashion garment-making, clothing, and
tailoring. He modified Berthold Akzidenz
Grotesk for the logo typeface. "Hopefully,
it will make it onto some sort of fashion
garment one day," he adds.

Client: **Pierre Darnton at Question Air**
Art Direction: **Dan Witchell**
Design: **Proud Creative**
Country: **UK**

## (Lucky) Loke

Loke is an exclusive denim label for men focusing on using the finest Japanese denim and clean, contemporary design on T-shirts, sweatshirts, and shirts. Proud Creative worked with Darnton in creating a new brand to appeal to Loke's specific market—cool, affordable clothes for modern Londoners. "We wanted it to feel like a quirky European brand," explains Witchell. "Pierre, who was fundamentally involved in the project, is Swedish and helped to create this mixed-up identity. Loke is the mythical fire giant/deity of mischief in Norse mythology, a son of the giants Fárbauti and Laufey. He is described as the 'contriver of all fraud.' Despite much research, the figure of Loke remains obscure." The logo has been applied to clothing, labels, leather, stationery, cards, and in store.

Client: **Graham & Brown**
Design: **Paul Reardon at Peter & Paul**
Country: **UK**

## Graham & Brown 60th Anniversary

Graham & Brown is renowned for its innovative wallpaper design, collaborating with designers such as Julien Macdonald, Laurence Llewelyn-Bowen, Linda Barker, and Wayne Hemingway. It wanted a logo to celebrate 60 years of producing innovative design, and manufacturing wallpaper and wall furnishings. "The idea was to illustrate elements of patterns created by Graham & Brown from past and present to form a typographic 60," explains Reardon. "All the elements were taken from the Graham & Brown archive and then simplified to work in the context of a logo." The logo was applied to a commemorative press box, letterhead, and all press material for 2006/2007.

Sixty years of
**GRAHAM & BROWN**

Client: **Revolve Clothing Company**
Design: **Paul Sych at Faith**
Country: **Canada**

## Peace

While Sych was designing a number of logos for Revolve, the company spotted one Sych had already created, and wanted it for a new line of clothing. "They thought it was appropriate for the clothing they had been producing at the time, and thought it would fit their audience and mandate," explains Sych. "It was based on a feeling of typography from the Middle East and customized as an English character set." The logo was applied to Revolve's apparel.

Client: **Blacks Visual Merchandising**
Art Direction: **Oliver Walker**
Design: **Ollystudio**
Country: **UK**

## Blacks VM

Blacks VM is a visual merchandise design, manufacturer, and installation company. Its clients include most major retailers as well as several smaller independents. The market in which Blacks VM operates is fiercely competitive and continually changing. Therefore, Walker's brief was to create a logo that would compete and last in this visually aware industry. The logo is composed of two separate elements: the word "Blacks" and the illustrative VM. "Blacks" is set in Helvetica Neue75, providing the logo with its "constant." A range of sans-serif fonts are used for the illustrative elements, depending on the final use. "Using strong typography as the basis of the identity allows it to speak about creativity without being specific to any one area of the company's trade alone. It also allows the identity to expand and ride above the changes and trends of the VM industry." explains Walker."

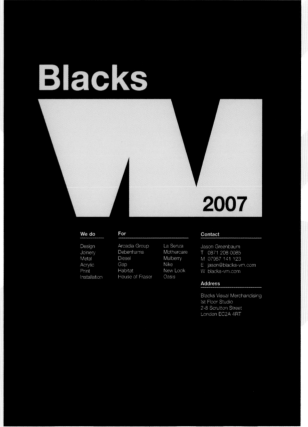

Client: **Atelier 99**
Design: **Marc Antosch at**
   **Tilt Design Studio**
Country: **France**

## Atelier 99

Atelier 99 produces customized men's shirts. Tilt Design Studio was commissioned to develop its corporate identity, including logo, business cards, hangtags, packaging, and online shop. "The client wanted a simple, clean, and fashion-like logo," explains Antosch. "We opted for using just type and no imagery or vector art. We wanted to create a very simple and modern logotype, with big fashion brands like Prada and Boss in mind—a logo immediately associated with 'fashion.' We did several proposals, but the client decided on this one because of its handmade touch."

Client: **Jeremy Brill**
Design: **Oscar Wilson at Studio Oscar**
Country: **UK**

## Brill

Brill previously traded under the name "Clerkenwell Music," selling CDs and vinyl, but with the rise in iPod/download culture, it needed to diversify to survive. So, it introduced the café element, which increased turnover and gave it the cache of a destination store. It commissioned Studio Oscar to create its new identity. "Using a script-style font was discussed from the outset," Wilson explains. "Also, the fact that the logo should be simple and have a classic, vintage feel to it." The resultant logo, featuring a slightly amended version of Freehand 575, has a distinct vintage America feel. It has been applied to neon signage, advertising, stickers, and on the web.

27 Exmouth Market, London, EC1R 4QL | 020 7833 9757 | jeremy@clerkenwellmusic.co.uk

Client: **Coop**
Design: **Chean Wei Law aka Undoboy/
Ryan Meis**
Country: **Malaysia/USA**

## Coop

Coop sells design goods including
T-shirts and toys from Undoboy and
Meis. "Through the logo, we wanted
to show the sense of collaboration
between two designers within Coop,"
explains Undoboy. "Our solution was
to incorporate a speech bubble into
the identity and use two different colors—
light blue and magenta—to represent
each of the designers." Undoboy and
Meis created the typeface together.
The logo has been applied to Coop
packaging and product booklets.

Client: **Wag Magazine**
Design: **Luca Marchettoni**
Country: **Italy**

## Wag Magazine

Wag Magazine is an experimental
magazine about visual communication.
Marchettoni was commissioned to create
the logo for its launch. "The goal was to
transmit the idea of a container of things
constantly moving and evolving, like the
magazine," he explains. "Something full
of stuff coming from all over the world,
taking the reader across loads of different
visual cultures and styles. We first came
up with an appropriate name, and then
designed a very simple typographic logo
for it." Its design was inspired by the
"TRANSWAGGON" writing found on
cargo train wagons.

Client: **Man Woman Girl Boy Magazine**
Design: **Brett Phillips at 3 Deep Design**
Country: **Australia**

## Garcon

3 Deep Design developed this logotype for the inaugural issue of <u>Man Woman Girl Boy</u> magazine. Two versions were developed (Dirty Boy and Clean Boy) because the magazine is in two parts. "We were asked to establish a masthead that was in keeping with the attitude and feel of the magazine," explains Phillips. "Youthful, fresh, and contemporary, each issue of the magazine will change in both form and content and as such, will require a bespoke approach to the development of this element." The logotype design was inspired by 3 Deep Design's fascination with notions of hyper-reality and fantasy. Given how the magazine is delivered to its audience, and its limited exposure in traditional newsstand environments, the logotype did not have to conform to the traditional modes of identification or clarification. With delivery of their own personal copy, each recipient's experience of the issue was more personal, timely, and considered.

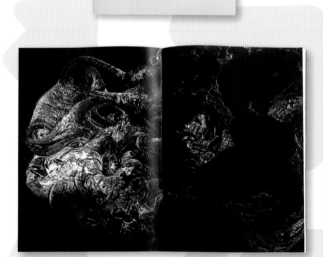

# PARIS PEOPLETTES
## *la capitale en super flux*

Client: **Paris Peoplettes**
Design: **Elisabeth Arkhipoff at Romantic Surf**
Country: **France**

## Paris Peoplettes

Paris Peoplettes is a website and city guide that records the daily lives of several women in diary form, including shopping, restaurants, and nightlife. Arkhipoff created an identity for the site using a modified Helvetica Neue. The geometric elements she added inside the letterforms are animated on the website to resemble traffic in the city. Harrington typeface was used for the subtitle text in order to soften and feminize the logo.

## Emmi Salonen, Emmi, UK

**What do you think makes a good logo?**
One that gives me a hint of what the company stands for before I even read the logotype. A logo that has character, like meeting an interesting person. One I get along with! Why? I suppose because I like logos that tell a story. I like clever solutions that show someone has spent time refining their ideas.

**Which are your favorite three logos?**
In order of creation, first, the Swiss flag. The cross has a long history and defining the mark has gone on for centuries. But it looks modern, as if it were designed today. The current use of the mark is beautiful through Swiss products, passport, etc. Second, the trademark to FW Purser by Fletcher Forbes Gill. I like the play with elements; initials with a visual twist that together create something new. The mark came about when a joiner was putting up shelves in the designers' studio and they wanted to explain to him what they did. Finally, Milton Glaser's NY logo label—I just love it.

**When approaching the design of a logo, what inspires you?**
The best is when the client or its product/company inspires you. If this is not immediate, I try to dig a bit deeper and find the inspiration within it. I start by writing down its key messages and words, and then see where that takes me.

**In some cases there are many places a logo may need to be applied—how much of a consideration is that when designing a logo?**
It's definitely something to bear in mind. A good logo should fulfill all its needs for applications. Sometimes a logo can be flexible enough to be site-specific; this can be a lovely thing to happen too.

**What is the most important job for a logo to do?**
To give the right first impression and keep good company as time moves on.

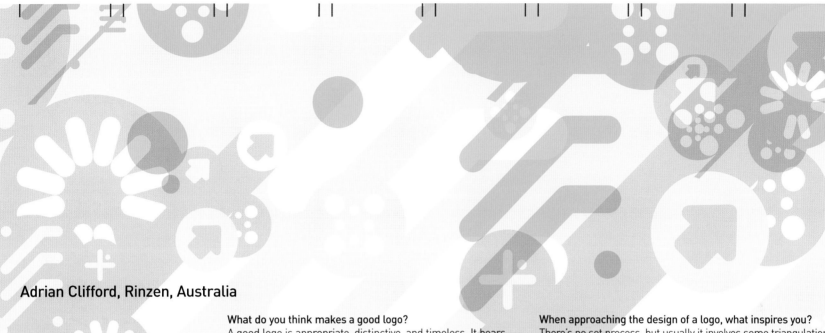

## Adrian Clifford, Rinzen, Australia

**What do you think makes a good logo?**
A good logo is appropriate, distinctive, and timeless. It bears the weight of its identity conclusively and indivisibly.

**Which are your favorite three logos?**
It's hard to pick absolute favorites, but these are among the much admired: Swiss flag—perfect proportions and color. I have no idea who designed it; the dimensions were formalized some time in the late 1800s. If you don't consider a flag a logo, then simply substitute the Red Cross logo—similarly perfect, as you'd expect since it's a conscious reversal of the Swiss national flag. The Copyleft logo—a brilliantly simple and communicative design, illustrates the conceptual re-evaluation of the idea of copyright elementally, like some sort of graphic judo throw. The original UPS logo—one of many branding milestones by Paul Rand. I mention this one in particular to raise the topic of the seemingly inexorable virus of classic logos being updated with ugly and unnecessary three-dimensionalization. The original was perfect—clarity, grace, and character, tied up in a neat bow.

**What has been your most successfully designed logo?**
It's impossible to choose just one. To us a successful logo is one that does its job and integrates seamlessly into the surrounding work—either by becoming an indivisible part of an illustrated work, or by doing all of the heavy lifting to communicate an idea or brand on its own. As long as it fulfills its function, it's no more or less successful than other logos we may have designed.

**When approaching the design of a logo, what inspires you?**
There's no set process, but usually it involves some triangulation of the key factors surrounding the project—the elements of character or pure idea that are inherent to the project/business being branded; the range of applications in which the logo needs to work; and the broader cultural milieu in which the project/business will exist, and to which the logo may be sympathetic or willfully contrary, depending on the desired outcome.

**In some cases there are many places a logo may need to be applied—how much of a consideration is that when designing a logo?**
It's a huge consideration, and is one of the reasons that a good logo design is usually constructed from the outset to present cleanly and boldly in a single color.

**What is the most important job for a logo to do?**
To introduce itself compellingly to the viewer in the tone and manner befitting the project or brand, whatever that may be.

03

"A logo creates a visual connection between its owner and the public—it must convey a message that tells the public what the company does."

**Oliver Walker, UK**

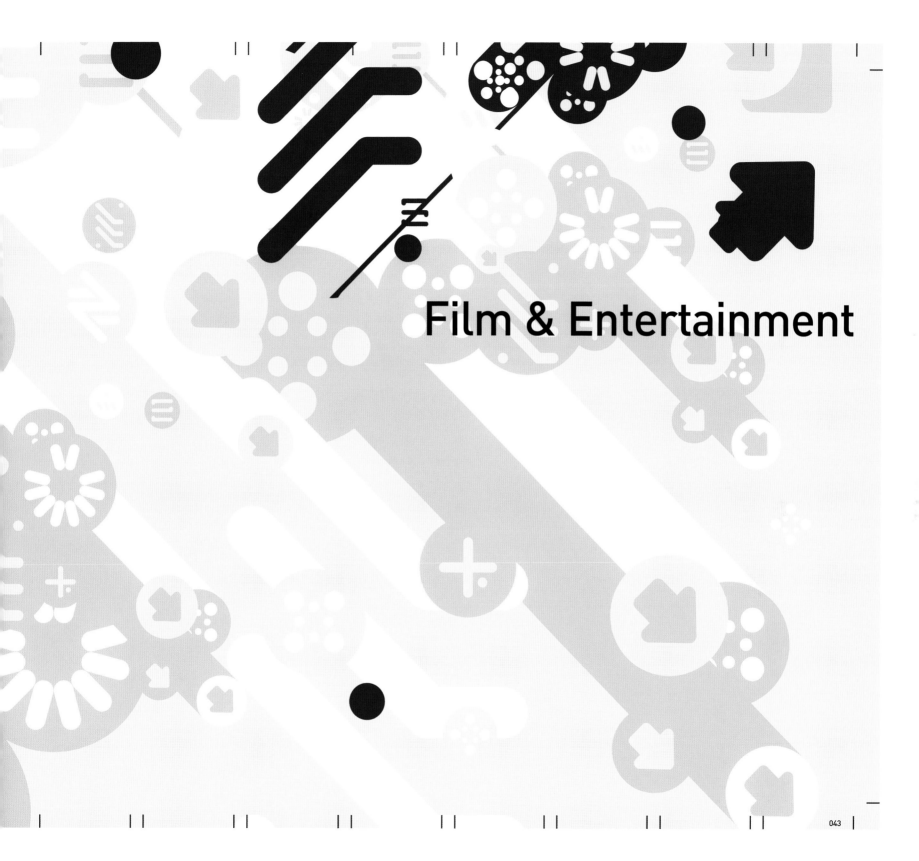

# Film & Entertainment

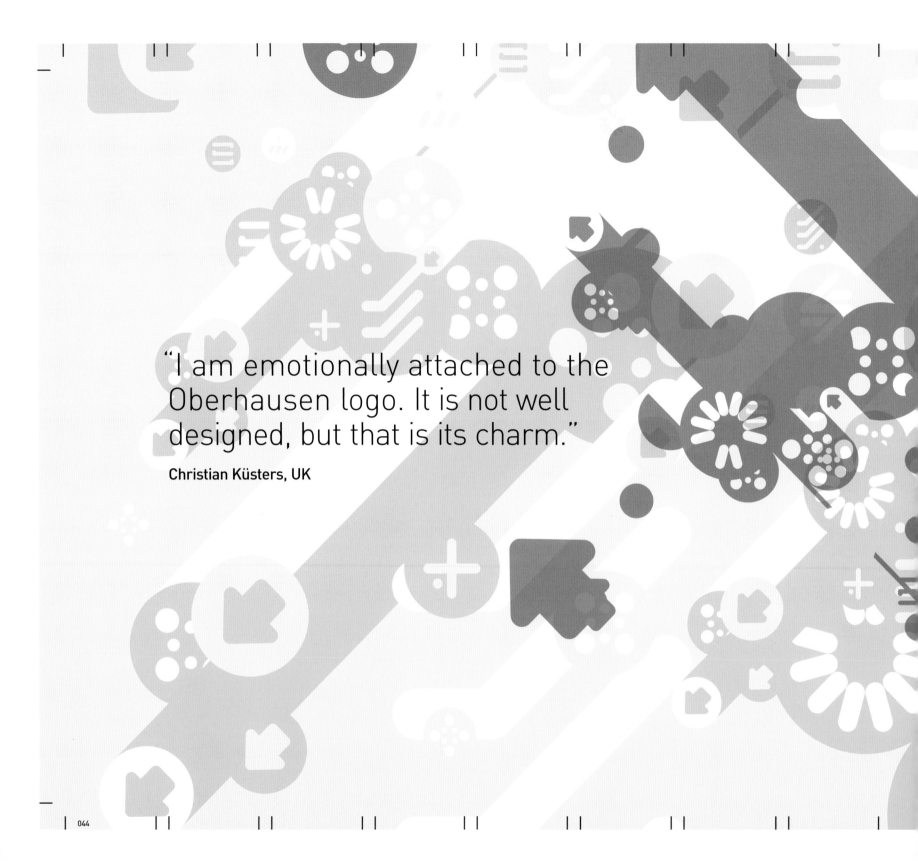

"I am emotionally attached to the Oberhausen logo. It is not well designed, but that is its charm."

**Christian Küsters, UK**

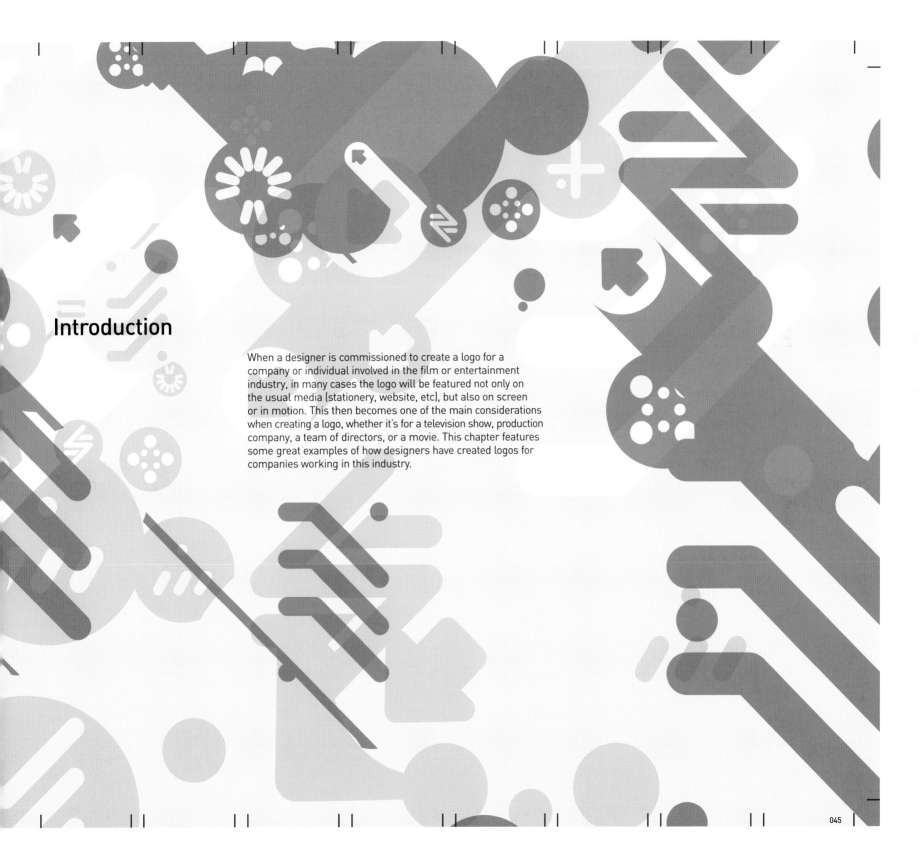

# Introduction

When a designer is commissioned to create a logo for a company or individual involved in the film or entertainment industry, in many cases the logo will be featured not only on the usual media (stationery, website, etc), but also on screen or in motion. This then becomes one of the main considerations when creating a logo, whether it's for a television show, production company, a team of directors, or a movie. This chapter features some great examples of how designers have created logos for companies working in this industry.

# The Fall

Client: **Tarsem at Treetop Films**
Design: **Stefan G. Bucher at 344 Design**
Country: **USA**

## The Fall

Bucher created this logo for fantasy movie The Fall by Tarsem. The movie was set in Los Angeles in the 1920s and expands into the rich and ornate fantasy world of a little girl and her silent-movie stuntman friend. "Tarsem didn't actually ask for a logo, but I made one for him as part of a book about the movie, which he had asked me to design," explains Bucher. "It felt to me that a logo was needed. When Tarsem saw it, he had his doubts. He prefers very minimal type, but all his trusted advisers fell in love with the logotype, so it stayed on the book. It also adorns the poster and leads of the opening titles of the movie itself." It is inspired by the fantasy sequences that take place in India. The logo plays off the ornate calligraphy seen in the movie, but stays connected to Bucher's minimal aesthetic. Modified Univers was used to create the logo.

Client: **Double Knot**
Design: **Stylo Design**
Country: **UK**

## Double Knot

Double Knot is an independent film production company specializing in music videos. Stylo Design created this logo using a bespoke typeface centered around the symbol of a double knot. The logo was applied across packaging, stationery, and marketing materials, in some instances using foil blocking and blind embossing.

Client: **This Is Network**
Design: **Tatiana Arocha**
Country: **USA**

## Network

This Is Network is a production company that focuses on design and animation. It wanted the simplicity of a classic corporate logo without feeling corporate. The goal was to create an image that was playful, with childlike simplicity, and draw inspiration from the television industry. "The inspiration for the logo was derived from the iconic image of TV color bars, turning a very conventional image into something new and fun, and creating a direct connection with the nature of the business, which is graphic design for television," explains Arocha. For the text, Arocha customized the Chalet typeface. The logo was applied to stationery, business cards (on which it was embossed), stickers, postcards, and on the website.

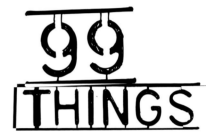

Client: **Fox Networks**
Design: **Ross Imms at A-Side Studio**
Country: **USA**

## 99 Things

Buster Design, a production house, commissioned A-Side Studio to create this logo for a Fox Networks show called 99 Things. The show counts down through 99 incidents on a specific theme, for example, 99 sleepwalking disasters, 99 stunts gone wrong, etc. With the help of a script and show synopsis, A-Side Studio developed a typographic solution. "The themes covered in the show were quite edgy, which we reflected in the typographic identity that we created," explains Imms. "We experimented with existing stencil fonts, but none of them processed the raw edge that we required, so we rendered one ourselves and applied it to our concepts for the show open and section divides."

Client: **YES Networks, Inc.**
Design: **Stefan G. Bucher at 344 Design**
Country: **USA**

## YES

YES is a cell-phone service that allows US listeners to find songs they have heard played within the past seven days on the US's top radio stations. It also allows listeners to rate currently playing songs to influence the charts, and to chat with other listeners. The brief was that the logo work at a very small pixel size on cell-phone browsers, and scale up well for use on promotional banners. It had to clearly communicate the cell-phone link and, ideally, entice people to dial the code to find out the track. "The logo references the look of a touch-tone phone," explains Bucher. VAG Rounded typeface was used to create the logo, which was embossed and debossed on business cards to suggest telephone buttons being pushed.

Client: **Loica**
Design: **Flavio Bagioli**
Country: **Chile**

## Loica

Bagioli received no written brief for this logo for Loica, a postproduction and visual effects company. "It was always a different instruction, given verbally. The requirements of the logo were never clear; the specific needs were very subjective, like it had to look good, have balance, and be readable from a distance. Just the basic common sense for any good logo," explains Bagioli. So, using a custom-made typeface, he created this lively logo which mixes the concept of abstract with color. "I was inspired by the multicolored combinations you see in native Latin American costumes," he adds. "The things you see in northern Chile, Bolivia, and Peru make the perfect color combinations." The logo has been used on CDs and DVDs, and also on the company website.

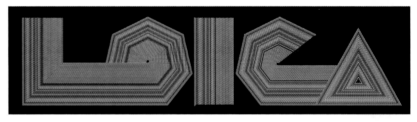

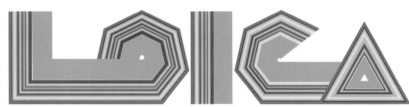

Client: **Cornwall Film Festival**
Design: **A-Side Studio**
Country: **UK**

## Cornwall Film Festival

Cornwall Film Festival (CFF) is an independent film festival, showcasing up-and-coming Cornish filmmakers, with an additional Surf Film Festival. The Cornish Chough icon is a motif that accompanies the CFF corporate identity, which takes on a different form each year. The brief to A-Side Studio was fairly open, so it used the chough, but decided to illustrate it in a contemporary style, symbolizing Cornish heritage and the festival's forward-thinking attitude. The bird template was filled with quick Illustrator doodles that represented "Cornwall" and "film." Intended only as a rough visual, the designers liked its innocent charm and used it for the final logo, which appeared on all the 2006 festival literature, including program, posters, fliers, and T-shirts.

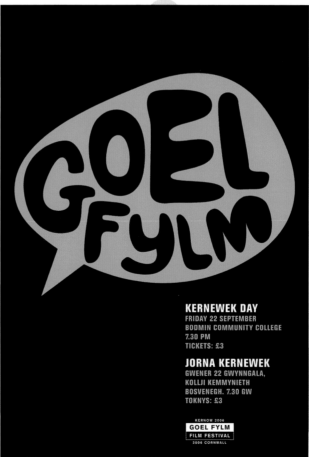

Client: **Sianel Pedwar Cymru**
Art Direction: **Dan Witchell**
Design: **Proud Creative**
Country: **UK**

## S4C

Welsh TV channel S4C asked Proud Creative to deveop its new identity. "The idea was simple really; we wanted to create a clean, memorable logo that would be instantly recognizable," explains Witchell. "We wanted to keep a strong visual connection to Wales. The new design emphasizes this with the 'C' for Cymru (Wales) separated from the 'S4' (Channel 4) by a forward slash. This mechanism also has another use. We felt that a modern identity should be a living thing so the /C can also be used to highlight an adjective, for example S4/Croeso, which is 'welcome' in English." The logo was drawn from scratch, but based on Typ1451. Proud Creative worked closely with Lineto to create a bespoke version of this font for S4C called S4C sans, which is used as its house font.

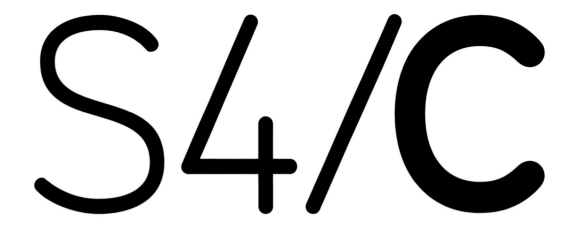

Client: **Frank D. Lanterman**
**Regional Center**
Design: **Geoff Kaplan at**
**General Working Group**
Country: **USA**

## Perspectives

Perspectives, an international film festival and forum, promotes understanding and the inclusion of people with developmental disabilities within the community. Kaplan's brief was to create a positive and vibrant logo. "The design was inspired by a visit to the Institut Musulman in Paris," he explains. "I was taken by the mosaics and moucharabiyahs; they suggested irises, similar to the way Jean Nouvel interpreted these forms in his Institut du Monde Arabe. Additionally, the kaleidoscopic forms suggested limitless potential and cinematic brilliance." Kaplan drew the logotype, and the secondary typefaces are Geometric 231 and 415.

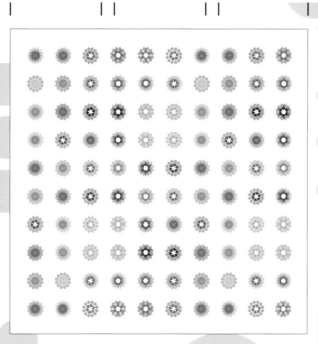

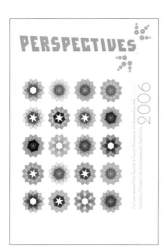

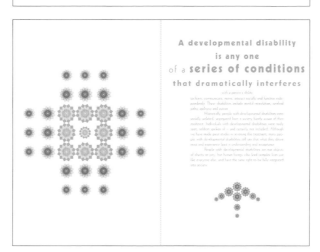

Client: **Sugar Factory**
Design: **Ivo Schmetz at 310k**
Country: **The Netherlands**

## Pop!

310k designed this logo for Pop!, a series of dance nights at the Sugar Factory club. "The idea behind the logo was to create a feeling that fits with the night; get a bit of the cocktail and champagne feeling mixed up with a pop culture and electro music style," explains Schmetz. The logo was applied to flyers, cocktail menus, and free-drink cards, which were screenprinted with gold on black.

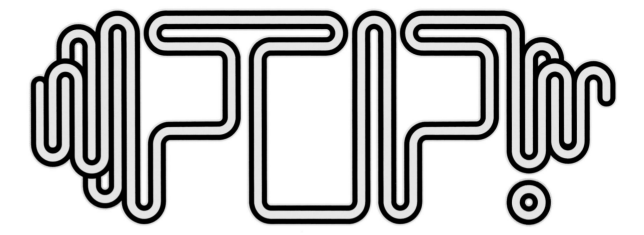

cocktail list

**cocktails** € 6.50

**PINA COLADA**
bacardi premium black, bacardi coco, coconut milk, pineapple juice, fresh pineapple

**MOJITO**
bacardi reserva, limes, cane sugar, mint leaves, crushed ice, soda water

**CAIPIRINHA**
cachaca, limes, cane sugar, crushed ice

**STRAWBERRY CAIPIRINHA**
cachaca, limes, cane sugar, fresh strawberries, crushed ice

**MARGARITA**
tequila, triple sec, lemon juice

**STRAWBERRY MARGARITA**
tequila, strawberry liqueur, lemon juice, fresh strawberries

**RASPBERRY RUMPUNCH**
bacardi razz, lime juice, sugar syrup, fresh raspberries, still water

**BANANA DAIQUIRI**
bacardi oro, sugar syrup, lemon juice, fresh banana

**MELON BALL**
republic vodka, melon liqueur, fresh melon, orange juice

**MARTINI DRY**
bombay sophire gin, dry martini, olive

**VODKATINI**
republic vodka, dry martini, olive

**ZERO PERCENT** non alcoholic
cranberry, pineapple, orange juice, lime juice and fresh fruit

**CAIPIRINHEE** non alcoholic
limes, cane sugar, mint leaves, ginger ale

**shooters** € 4.50

**SUGAR DADDY**
vodka, kahlua, galliano

**PIPSQUEAK**
frangelico, vodka, lemon juice

**FLATLINER**
tequila gold, sambuca, tabasco

**SHIT ON THE GRASS**
sambuca, creme de menthe

**EMBRYO**
cognac, kahlua, baileys

Client: **Pentas Project**
Design: **Chean Wei Law aka Undoboy**
Country: **Malaysia**

## Pentas Project

Pentas Project is a performing arts society that specializes in drama, and collaborates with different artists for each project. Its logo is based on two squares, to represent a stage and the artists who perform on it. "A square was the perfect form to use to represent a platform, or stage, and another small square inside it creates the feeling of it being centralized and steady," explains Undoboy. Esbits typeface was chosen to continue the visual theme of squares.

Client: **Fatastar Productions**
Design: **Luca Marchettoni**
Country: **Italy**

## Fatastar

Fatastar Productions offers production and postproduction services for promos, music videos, and commercials. Through its logo, it wanted to communicate three basic concepts: youth, fantasy, and energy. "The idea was to create something related to dreams, something energetic and playful," explains Marchettoni. "The main inspiration comes from Little Nemo, the main character in a fabulous series of American comic strips by Winsor McCay. The stories told in the comics are all about the dreams of this kid. I've always been a great fan of him." The logo was used on business and corporate identity, and promotional materials, including some garments.

Client: **Locals**
Design: **Michael Mandrup/Bandage**
Countries: **Denmark/Germany**

## Locals

Locals, a Hamburg-based commercial director duo, commissioned Mandrup to create a humorous logo. "I decided to think of Locals as some far-out, western, isolated thing," explains Mandrup. "So local that it had become inbred. And the outcome was this two-headed cowboy monster, which fitted nicely with the fact that this was a duo, performing as one director." Mandrup drew the letters in rope as though the character were holding a lasso, in keeping with the monster cowboy theme. The logo was used for DVD covers, CD covers, and on business cards.

Client: **Paul Pope**
Design: **Rilla Alexander at Rinzen**
Country: **Germany**

## THB

THB is a comic series written, drawn, and published by New York–based comics auteur Paul Pope. Its name, THB, is the name of the comic's main character, a synthetic android, or "mek," and is an acronym for his chemical composition Tri-Hydro-Bioxygenate. Rinzen was commissioned to create a new logo for the comic in 2003, in the run-up to the publication of the Giant THB 1.v.2 issue. "There was a long period of discussion leading up to the creation of the logo," explains Alexander, "centering on the various aesthetic and thematic ideas at play in the comic itself. Paul describes the THB series as 'an Arabic western set on Mars.' The logo is a synthesis of the different cultural touchstones indicated by that phrase: Arabic-flavored Mars society, Paul's love of classic western logo design, rock-and-roll energy, and sci-fi futurism. The Martian aspects of the logo are echoes of calligraphic Martian writing seen in the THB comics." The logo also references the "trimolecular" nature of the THB character himself, with three circular molecule shapes apparent in endpoints of the T, H, and B letterforms.

Client: **MTV Networks**
Design: **A-Side Studio**
Country: **USA**

### Does This Look Infected?

This logo was commissioned for MTV Networks by Buster Design, a production house. Designed for an educational show on an established network, it required a playful aesthetic. A-Side Studio created the logo with a hand-drawn typeface and background. The logo was designed specifically for on-screen use, and for the US market.

09.25.03/ GIANT THB 1.V.2/ 96 PGS/ NEW COMICS ENERGY
MEK-POWERED FOR NEW ACCELERATION/ SEE PAULPOPE.COM FOR MORE

Client: **Kiss FM/Emap Performance**
Design: **Simon Glover at ODD**
Country: **UK**

# KISS

Despite its well-respected foundations of piracy and cutting-edge behavior, Kiss's enduring "super-youth" credentials suffered following the massive rise of the iPod-fueled music revolution. It needed to adapt quickly and reconnect with the new cultural mainstream, while maintaining its cutting-edge brand reputation. ODD's goal was to transform Kiss from a radio station to an entertainment brand. "In its most simplistic form, the new identity places emphasis on the Kiss 'K' and creates an iconic symbol for the Kiss brand," explains Glover. "But along with a new positioning and manifesto, we also wanted it to reflect the same confidence and heritage as the Nike swoosh or Apple mark—something kids would draw in sketch pads, clubs would project on walls, and music journalists and listeners would use and recognize as a symbol of endorsement." Inspired by origami, the resultant identity exists in both its static form, and as an animated element, including advertising in print and TV, for the radio station, cell-phone content, online, and in 3-D form as on-air lightboxes.

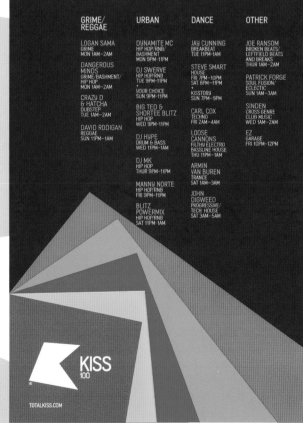

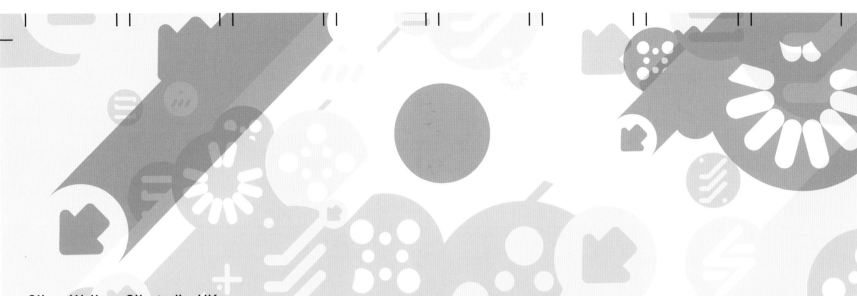

## Oliver Walker, Ollystudio, UK

**What do you think makes a good logo?**
Ownership and authority are key elements in any logo—who owns it, does it clearly state who it represents, does it have the authority, simplicity, and clarity to avoid confusion with any other organization or be misleading in any way? A logo creates a visual connection between its owner and the public—it must convey a message that tells the public what the company does.

**Which are your favorite three logos?**
Nike. Some say the Nike "swoosh," some say the Nike "tick," but in fact the Nike logo design is an abstract wing designed by Carolyn Davidson in 1971 for $35. This simple, solid corporate logo design was registered as a trademark in 1995. It is perhaps one of the best logos ever to be designed as it suggests all the key elements that sum up Nike and what it represents. It does this with beauty, simplicity, strength, and fun. There can't be many people in the world who don't recognize it. The Warner Communications logo. This beautiful logo was designed by Saul Bass & Associates in 1972. It is a classic example of the corporate identity program introduced to unite all of the satellite companies that made up Warner Communications. Based around the W of the old, the WB shield in the new logo was rounded and more modern-looking, with a digital feel to express the modern communications company that Warner had become. It was ahead of its time in terms of style, it stood the test of time, and it still inspires many logos. My third is the old Kone Lifts logo which, unfortunately, I know nothing about. I saw it almost every day on the side of the company vans. Every time I saw it, it brought a smile to my face. I can draw it for you in seconds, and it will tell you exactly what they do. This logo has all the key elements mentioned above, and its staggering simplicity makes me wish that I had designed it.

**What has been your most successfully designed logo?**
Sports Internet Group, designed for the first global online betting company in 1999. It offered online betting facilities across the world, so the design had to represent sport to customers in every country. The two major considerations were that it be suitable for on-screen use, and that it could be adapted to be specific to one sport. The company was so successful that William Hill bought it after eight months, but unfortunately the name Sports Internet Group was buried.

**When approaching the design of a logo what inspires you?**
You start by finding out exactly what your client does and what its aspirations are—you do an audit. The fun then starts by exploring all the different ways in which you can represent your findings. Basically, a successful logo is the result of intense thought and hard work.

**In some cases there are many places a logo may need to be applied—how much of a consideration is that when designing a logo?**
The most important thing to get right is the visual representation, the clarity, and the simplicity. Application is always in the back of your mind, but it is not the first priority.

**What is the most important job for a logo?**
The ability to communicate to its audience, to conjure up an image of the organization it represents.

# Christian Küsters, CHK Design, UK

**What do you think makes a good logo?**
Here is the logo entry from Wikipedia, which pretty much sums it up. "A typical logo is designed to cause immediate recognition by the viewer. The logo is one aspect of the brand of a company or economic entity, and the shapes, colors, fonts, and images are usually different from others in a similar market. Logos may also be used to identify organizations or other entities in noneconomic contexts. Logo design is commonly believed to be one of the most important areas in graphic design, thus making it the most difficult to perfect. The logo, or brand, is not just an image, it is the embodiment of an organization. Because logos are meant to represent companies and foster recognition by consumers, it is counterproductive to redesign logos often."

**Which are your favorite three logos?**
The Bauhaus logo, for intellectual reasons. It was designed by Oskar Schlemmer in 1922. I like how the Bauhaus philosophy—reducing a thing to its bare essentials, whether this be a building, a piece of furniture, a painting—influenced the visual outcome, in this case a human head. I also like the Bauhaus lettering on the exterior of the Walter Gropius building, but the Oskar Schlemmer logo design is slightly more unusual. The Oberhausen logo, for emotional reasons. It was impossible to find out who designed this logo. The design is simply a sans-serif, uppercase, bold italic "O" followed by a full stop. It was the first time I recognized a logo as such, and, growing up in Oberhausen, I became emotionally attached to it. It is definitely not well designed, but that is its charm. The Deutsche Bank logo—designed by Anton Stankowski in 1974. It is one of my favorites because it seems to sum up the essence of what a bank is about: security and progress. The logo seems to effortlessly combine those two factors.

**What has been your most successfully designed logo?**
Probably the redesign of the AD Architectural Design magazine logo. What makes it successful is that it combines all the factors a good logo needs. It is instantly recognizable, even before you actually read it. Yet, it clearly says "AD." As its design is based on one of the most archetypical architectural principles, I think it ages very well. It was designed in 1999.

**When approaching the design of a logo what inspires you?**
I usually start with the context and where the logo comes from. For AD Architectural Design I explored basic architectural principles, like squares, circles, and triangles. What inspires me is to try to find one or two essential points of the subject matter I am dealing with, and distill these into the logo. Stylistically the two magazine logos for AD Architectural Design and Miser & Now are on opposite ends of the design spectrum: one is constructed and very controlled, the other is very ornamental, but both logos work well within their specific contexts.

**In some cases there are many places a logo may need to be applied—how much of a consideration is that when designing a logo?**
It is obviously something to consider, but ultimately the logo is the idea/concept. Once the basic idea/concept has been established, it is then a matter of transferring that particular idea into the various media.

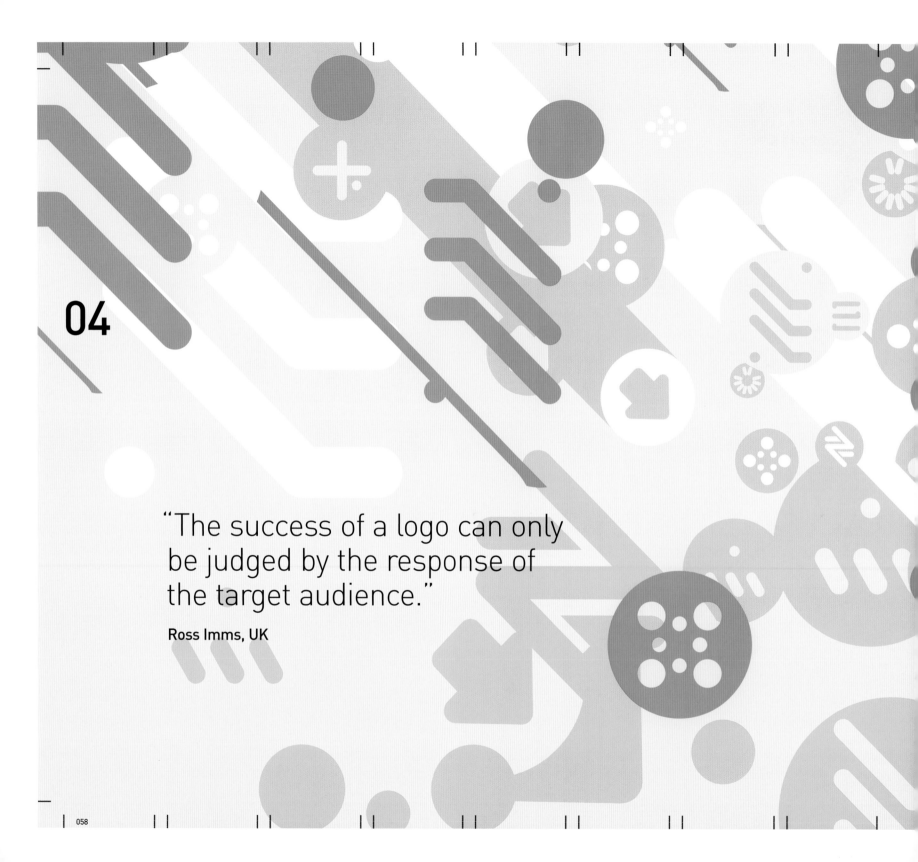

04

"The success of a logo can only be judged by the response of the target audience."

Ross Imms, UK

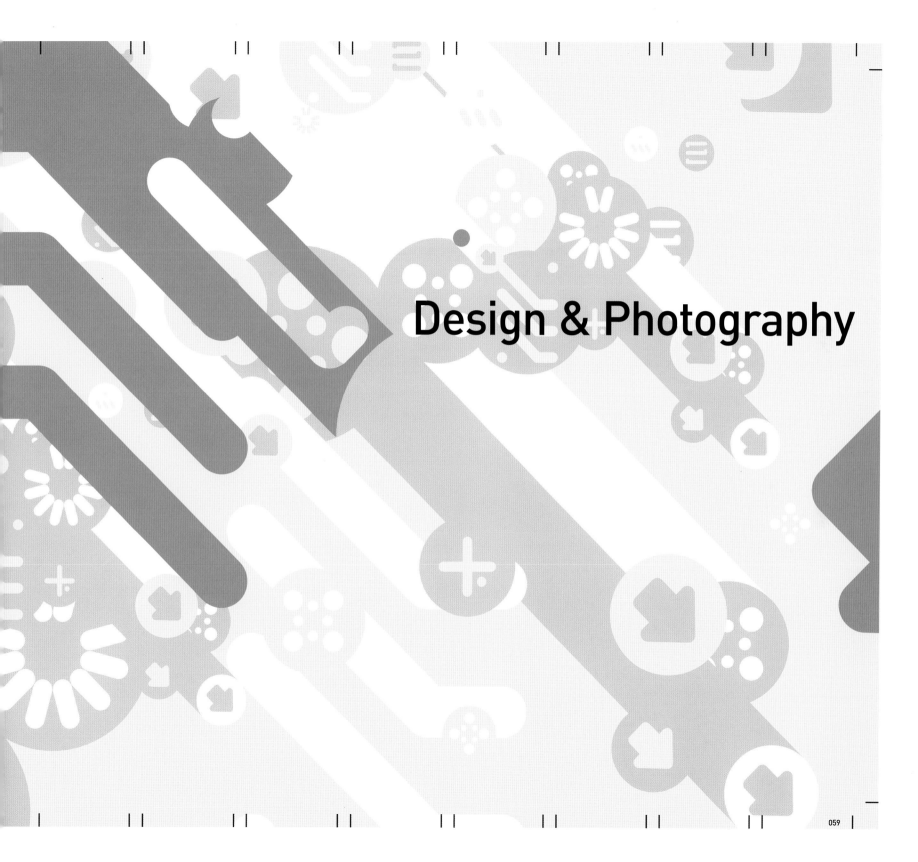

Design & Photography

"A good logo sticks in my mind and my mind doesn't mind it sticking there."

**Stefan Sagmeister, USA**

# Introduction

This is one of my favorite chapters in terms of the overall
collective style of the logo designs featured within it.
Developing logos for creative industries, including design
agencies, photographers, galleries, and exhibitions, can often
involve a more pared-down aesthetic. Often logos for design
agencies must not lean too much toward a certain style, but
rather be representative of all styles. The aim of galleries and
exhibitions is to appeal to a wide and varied public, so their
logos must be all-encompassing. And with photographers,
well, there is no general rule, but their logos tend to be more
experimental and often playful.

# AMELIA TROUBRIDGE

# addicted to drawing

Client: **Amelia Troubridge**
Design: **Ben Cave and Paul Jenkins at Ranch**
Country: **UK**

## Amelia Troubridge

Amelia Troubridge, a well-established photographer, commissioned Ranch to create her logo, the driving force behind which was the development of her new website. "The aim of the logo was to reflect Amelia's strong personality and strong photographic style," explains Cave. "We wanted the logo to be bold, but with character and a touch of quirkiness. The chosen typeface, ITC Grouch, captured this perfectly, along with having aesthetics sympathetic to the sectors that Amelia operates in, such as magazine and fashion photography. The monochromatic color scheme was a must—black is very much Amelia's color." The logo was applied to the website, stationery, portfolio, portfolio tags, and postcards.

Client: **Plugzine No. 2**
Design: **milkxhake**
Country: **Hong Kong**

## Addicted to Drawing

Addicted to Drawing was a project initiated by Plugzine, a bookazine issued annually. Plugzine invited different artists and designers from around the world (including China, Japan, the UK, and the USA) to design a specific logotype for each issue based on its editorial theme. The "broken pencil" logotype here is by milkxhake.

Client: **Daniel Goddemeyer**
Design: **Daniel Goddemeyer**
Country: **UK**

## Magic Book

This logo was designed for an interactive book project that Goddemeyer created online while studying for his MA at the Royal College of Art, London. "I wanted to create a logo that resembled the excitement and magic associated with the interactive book," he explains. The logo is based on the Platelet typeface; Goddemeyer used several hand-drawn stars around it to emphasize the "magic" element of the book.

Client: **Keith Talent Gallery**
Design: **Christian Küsters at CHK Design**
Country: **UK**

## Year_06

The Keith Talent Gallery, named after the main protagonist in Martin Amis' London Fields, exhibits the work of established artists alongside upcoming ones. It has housed over 30 exhibitions and organized its first art fair in 2006. It approached Küsters to design the overall visual identity, including the name, for this new annual London art event, which played host to 32 galleries from Europe and the USA. "It seemed to make sense to name the fair after the year in which it takes place," explains Küsters. "Consequently, the design of the logo is based on a changeable, but recognizable template." The logo is based on a matrix, which displays a new number each year, and is an integral part of the overall identity.

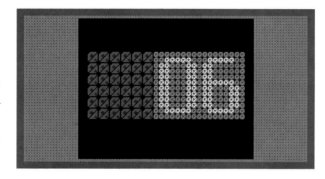

Client: **Paris-Ateliers**
Design: **Atelier Michel Bouvet/**
 **Odile Chambaut/Ellen Zhao**
Country: **France**

## Paris-Ateliers

Paris-Ateliers is an association that organizes classes for amateur artists in a professional setting. It commissioned Bouvet, Chambaut, and Zhao to create a logo that referred both to the traditional and modern aspects of studio arts, and that was inviting and recognizable through different applications (on stationery, membership cards, posters, signage, etc). The result is a simple, yet modern logo that can act as a stamp or signature mark for the company. The typeface used is Solex by Émigré.

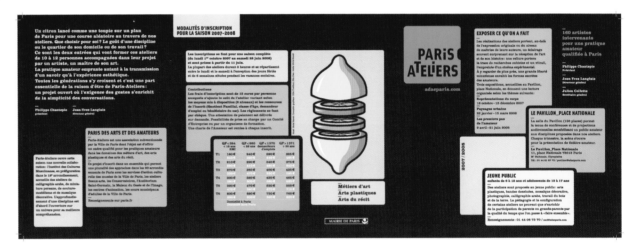

Client: **PMKFA**
Design: **Micke Thorsby at PMKFA**
Countries: **Japan/UK**

## PMKFA "Gold & Ice"

This self-promotional logo is a cut-and-paste graphic. "I was inspired by 'cheap' hip-hop typography and wanted to do something similar, but with a twist to make it more stylish," explains Thorsby. "In the end I chose to use the black-and-white version instead of the full-color one as it was more unclear in its language. Black-and-white logos often struggle to be as simple as possible; this one has simple main shapes, but with a very detailed 'filling.'" The type, Fleskfarsan, is one of PMKFA's typefaces. It features on the company's website, on a limited-edition T-shirt, and on the PMKFA catalog published by Gallery Vallery in Barcelona.

Client: **Pilotprojekt**
Design: **Alexander Egger**
Country: **Austria**

## Pilotprojekt

Pilotprojekt is a gallery space designed to enable graphic design creatives and the industry to connect. It commissioned Egger to create its identity—two lines and two circles used together to form the letters "PP." "I was inspired by historical references to minimalism, Bauhaus, and constructivism, so the whole identity is quite minimal and reduced," explains Egger. "The aim is for the circle and line element to be usable in conjunction with the full company name, as well as on its own as a marque." In keeping with the minimal theme, everything has been produced in black and white, with Helvetica typeface.

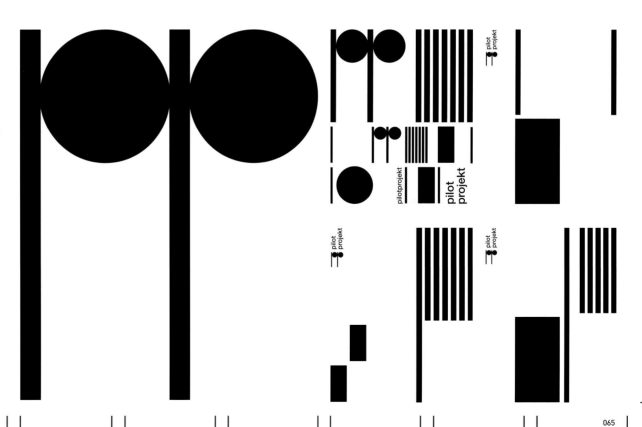

Client: **Purple Haze Studio**
Design: **Clemens Baldermann at**
**Purple Haze Studio**
Country: **Germany**

## Purple Haze

Purple Haze is a multidisciplinary graphic design studio that works for public and private clients on a variety of national and international projects (including expertise in conception, art direction, typography, design, and illustration). It produces communication solutions for print and packaging, brand applications, publishing, exhibitions, and websites. "As I am my own client, it is an infinite resource to experience and play around with the company identity," explains Baldermann. "It is a constant challenge to create new type forms or new constellations. With this in mind, and also being in a constantly changing process, it is difficult to focus on one logotype. Instead, I created a collection of logos assembled over time." For the logos, inspiration came mostly from former design eras across all genres. All the logotypes have been created using in-house custom-made fonts.

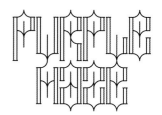

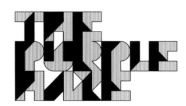
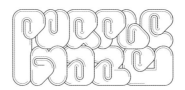

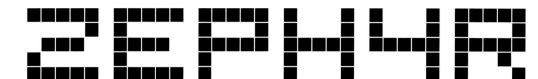

# C4.9 ZEPH4R

Client: **ZEPHYR Raum für Fotografie**
Design: **Jonas Grossmann at env design**
Country: **Germany**

## ZEPHYR

ZEPHYR is an exhibition space for international contemporary photography associated with the Reiss-Engelhorn-Museum Group in Mannheim. Grossmann's brief was for the logo to be contemporary, modern, and urban. Mannheim is based on a grid system—a plan of squares with no street names, but instead a matrix of letters and numbers. The client name ZEPHYR is a play on words; the address of the exhibition space is C4, which is pronounced as "zephyr" is in German. As a result, the logotype is based on a matrix of squares. The logo has been applied to fliers, invitations, posters, advertising, and catalogs.

Client: **Leonard Street Gallery**
Art Direction: **Phil Sims**
Design: **Neighbour**
Country: **UK**

## Leonard Street Gallery

Leonard Street Gallery, a contemporary art gallery, commissioned Neighbour to create its identity. The brief was to design an unconventional and progressive identity, while still retaining the authority of an art gallery. "The fundamental logo was designed as a formal, 'established art gallery' identity," explains Sims. "In order to fulfill the brief, we needed to introduce a secondary element to provide a fluid, ever-changing aspect to the branding. We achieved this by allocating each exhibition at the gallery its own color scheme, and overprinting the typography each time, disfiguring and obscuring the logo." The intention is that the logo is always overprinted with text or imagery. The typeface used for the main logo is Franklin Gothic Condensed, with Avant Garde as the secondary typeface.

Client: **THS**
Design: **Stefan Claudius**
Country: **Germany**

## THS

Claudius designed this logo for Thomas Schostok, a fellow designer and friend. Together they run the Cape Arcona Type Foundry, but they also work independently as graphic designers and artists. The type-only logo includes brackets, which were a feature of Schostok's previous logo, but have been made to look very different in this new version. "I wanted to give the logo a handwritten character and feel, so I drew the lettering," explains Claudius. "In fact, Thomas is now signing his paintings by hand with this logo." The logo has also been used on Schostok's stationery, website, promotional material, T-shirts, and jackets.

Client: **Blokk**
Art Direction: **Dan Witchell**
Design: **Proud Creative**
Country: **UK**

## Blokk

Blokk, an architecture practice, works on both commercial and residential projects. It commissioned Proud Creative to develop an ambiguous identity that was international in tone. "Our brief was to create a brand that represented their unique attitude to architecture and design," explains Witchell. "To this end the logo was designed to represent architecture in a very fundamental way. Going back to basics, we started to think about childhood and how we all start out with some sort of building skills. We wanted to represent this by having a modular design that could move around and still be recognizable as its brand." The logo has been applied to stationery (foil blocked and litho printed) and signage (machine-cut from polystyrene).

Client: **Accept & Proceed**
Design: **Various**
Country: **Global**

## A&P by...

Accept & Proceed, founded in 2006 by David Johnston, is a design and art direction facility providing print and interactive design for a wide range of sectors including the music, fashion, and advertising industries. Creative experimentation is at its core, as is the continual development of both personal and collaborative noncommercial projects. A&P by... is Johnston's ongoing side project for which he has asked several designers, illustrators, photo-graphers, and moving-image specialists to design a logo for A&P. These logos feature on Accept & Proceed's website, and appear randomly on each visit. Aside from using only black/white/grayscale and representing A&P in some way, there is no brief, allowing contributors to work as they do best, uninhibited by direction. Each of the designers featured has a link to their website so the project also works as an alternative links page.

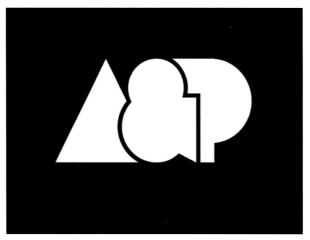

Client: **Kristen Whittle**
Design: **David Bennett at This Studio**
Country: **UK**

## Kristen Whittle

Architect Kristen Whittle commissioned This Studio to design his business identity with an open brief. "I looked at drawings and photos that he supplied and picked up on the architectural monospace typefaces he used in the annotations," explains Bennett. "From there I created a bespoke marque using Monospace 821 typeface designed by Bitstream." That font is now used as the main typeface in all Whittle's communications.

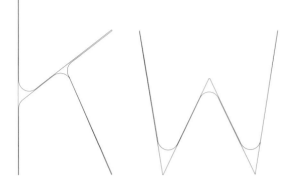

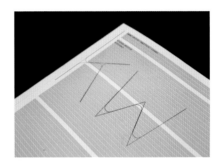

Client: **The Artment**
Design: **Lobby Design**
Country: **Sweden**

## The Artment

The Artment represents a new way of buying fine art. Founded in 2006, its objective is to get good-quality art into European homes. Lobby Design's early involvement with The Artment included making its logo, the idea of which focuses on the red dots found in galleries to mark favorite paintings or drawings. The dots have been used to create a series of circles in which to place the company's name. The logo, which uses Futura typeface, has been applied to all parts of the graphic identity, from stationery to stickers, to the company's website.

Client: **Peter Orevi**
Design: **Jonas Hellström at Lobby Design**
Country: **Sweden**

## Peter Orevi

Peter Orevi is a well-known fashion and advertising photographer. "Orevi didn't want the logo to be dull and stiff," explains Hellström. "He wanted the logotype to express his personality and the playfulness that he thrives on in his own creations. To suggest this playfulness, we started making variations of hand-made logos. When we finally got the right feeling for the name, we added a dash of insanity." The logo has been applied to Orevi's stationery, stickers, and website.

Client: **Ben Morris**
Design: **Emmi Salonen at Emmi**
Country: **UK**

## Pleasant Studio

The Pleasant Studio building suffered bomb damage during WWII. The aim of this identity was to reflect the story of the bomb through the use of different fonts, with one letter "breaking the grid." Avant Garde typeface, with an "A" customized by Salonen, was used to achieve this. The logo has been applied to the studio's stationery, brochure, and website.

Client: **Wilson Brothers**
Design: **Oscar Wilson at Studio Oscar**
Country: **UK**

## Wilson Brothers

Wilson Brothers is an umbrella name for family projects by Graphic Designer Oscar Wilson, 3-D Designer Ben Wilson, and Music Producer Luke Wilson. The brothers have worked together on projects including a hand-built fixed-wheel bicycle for Nike, and furniture for Stussy in Japan. They wanted a logo, designed by Studio Oscar, to accompany their collective work. As can be seen from the result, they were not concerned that it be immediately readable. "Various versions were made, and a family of logos exists," explains Wilson. "These are sometimes used as typographic repeats, making the logo even harder to read than usual." A new typeface was designed for the logo, which has been used across advertising, stickers, and the web, and was also laser-etched onto leather decals for the Nike bike.

Client: **InterAccess Electronic Media Arts Centre**
Design: **Clea Forkert at Underline Studio**
Country: **Canada**

## InterAccess Electronic Media Arts Centre

InterAccess is a not-for-profit, artist-run center that enables artists and the general public to explore the intersections of art and technology. It commissioned Underline Studio to redesign its logo with a brief for it simply to be "beautiful." "We were inspired by the imagery of cables, which was an extension of its previous logo, and a metaphor for much of what InterAccess does, not only in electronic media with its 'real' cables, but also as a link between artists, the public, media art, and artists' spaces," explains Forkert. "The flowing lines of the symbol reflect the connections that the center strives to promote, both globally and locally." The letterforms of the IA symbol were illustrated in-house, and the symbol has been used with Foundry Gridnik typeface.

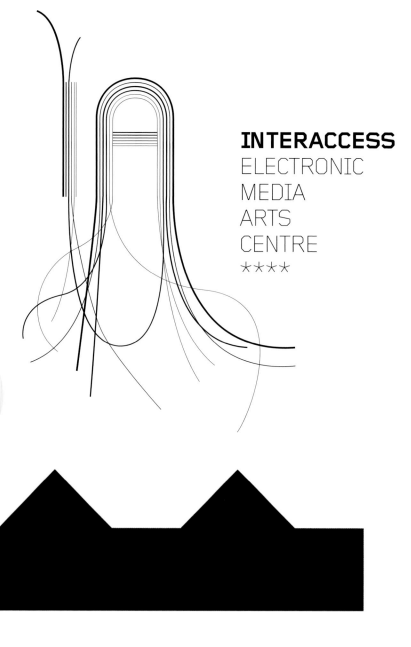

**INTERACCESS**
ELECTRONIC
MEDIA
ARTS
CENTRE
✶✶✶✶

Client: **Michelle Letelier**
Design: **Flavio Bagioli**
Countries: **Chile/Germany**

## Nowhere

Bagioli designed this logo for the Chilean video artist Michelle Letelier, who is now based in Berlin. Letelier wanted to set up a website with personal works. Bagioli explains, "For her logo, we started by trying to think of a name. We came up with "Nowhere" because a lot of her videos are about the non-place—lost spaces in cities, loneliness, and infinite open landscapes in the desert. Also, we thought about how everyone has the idea of having a home and builds their lives based on a home. We wanted to achieve the opposite to the classic idea of a living space with roof, doors, and windows. This is how the idea of a no home came out, a black home with a circle as a door and no roof." The logo (using Helvetica Neue Compressed Bold typeface) has been used in exhibitions, catalogs, and on Letelier's website, videos, and DVDs.

**NOWHERE**

Client: **310k**
Design: **Ivo Schmetz at 310k**
Country: **The Netherlands**

## 310k

310k specializes in graphic design, websites, video, and music, and organizes several different events. "We try to create a new logo every once in a while to reflect the new things we create," explains Schmetz. "For us it's not important to have the same logo for many years; we'd rather be flexible and change it from time to time." The logo has been applied to buttons, stickers, and T-shirts.

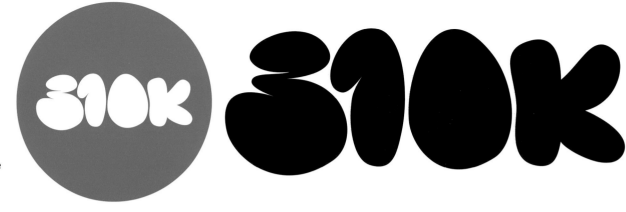

Client: **Emmi**
Design: **Emmi Salonen at Emmi**
Country: **UK**

## With Love

Emmi created this logo for her design studio. "I needed a mark I could use in correspondence with clients; on envelopes, e-mails, and promotional material," explains Salonen. "The idea for it came from wanting a rubber stamp for the studio that could be used on all mail leaving the studio. It grew from there and I now use it on badges, posters, and other items that we produce." The "With Love" stands for delivering good design, with good ethics and enjoyment.

Client: **Studio Jens Assur**
Design: **Jonas Banker at BankerWessel**
Country: **Sweden**

# STUDIO JENS ASSUR

## Studio Jens Assur

Jens Assur is one of Sweden's most famous documentary photographers. He has made several photographic reportages worldwide as well as a feature-length movie. Assur wanted an inventive, reliable, and simple logo, and gave BankerWessel two words he thought described his vision for the company: charm and demand. "First of all we wanted the logo to be recognizable and easy to use," explains Banker. "Studio Jens Assur is not afraid of having a strong, almost political opinion, so we wanted the logo to signal great self-confidence." The logo can be interpreted as an image of a flag, a political symbol, and a symbol of conquest. It uses Trade Gothic Bold No2 typeface.

STUDIO JENS ASSUR

BRÄNNKYRKAGATAN 16, SE-118 20 STOCKHOLM, SWEDEN  STUDIO +46 8 644 44 40  INFO@STUDIOJENSASSUR.COM  WWW.STUDIOJENSASSUR.COM

STUDIO JENS ASSUR

STUDIO JENS ASSUR

STUDIO JENS ASSUR

STUDIO JENS ASSUR

STUDIO JENS ASSUR

WWW.STUDIOJENSASSUR.COM

# mezzanine

Client: **Alice Euphemia**
Design: **Ariel Aguilera and Andrea Benyi**
    at **Pandarosa**
Country: **Australia**

## Mezzanine

Mezzanine gallery specializes in jewelry-based artworks. For the logo, "there was no real direction in the brief; the client left us to come up with a solution," explain Aguilera and Benyi. "Their only request was to create something with a timeless essence, and that reflected the style of the gallery space. We kept noticing the number nine within the name of the gallery so we decided to concentrate on this. After some research, we were amazed at the various meanings the number nine has in different cultures. It was seen as the perfect number by always equalling itself, i.e. $9 \times 9 = 81$, $8 + 1 = 9$. We took on this newfound knowledge and created a continuous type-based logo, which could be used as a repeated pattern." This concept of continuity was applied to gallery invitations (when put next to each other, these created a continuous pattern), and was also carried through to the poster applications.

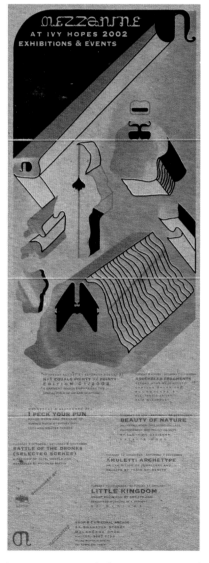

Client: **Alan Cook**
Design: **David Bennett at This Studio**
Country: **UK**

## Alan Cook

When photographer Alan Cook visited Bennett at This Studio to show his work, the two discussed creating his logo. "I was commissioned to create a completely new logo; nothing existed before, which was great," explains Bennett. "I presented just the one logo and he went with it, then I changed it completely about two weeks later. There was no real brief, but we wanted to create a system for his logo. Also we wanted to use words instead of numbers, so the telephone number was written out as words." The logo is set in ITC Avant Garde Bold and was applied to mailers sent out by Cook, as well as on his website and other communication.

**alan cook
photography
zero.seven.nine.seven.six
eight.one.five.four.six.four**

**www.
afcook.co.uk
email
alan@afcook.co.uk**

Client: **Undoboy**
Design: **Chean Wei Law aka Undoboy**
Country: **USA**

## Undoboy

Undoboy is a graphic design studio specializing in interactive, graphic, and character design, illustration, motion graphics, and toy design. "My studio embraces a simple philosophy—design brings happiness—which gave me a clear direction when I was processing the design," explains Undoboy. Inspired by Chinese characters and the Yin/Yang symbol, Undoboy created a colorful typographic logo, each letter of which is like an individual character. "I created little icons to bring a sense of humor and interaction to the studio identity, and to bring out an optimistic and joyous atmosphere," he adds.

Client: **Platform Artists Group Inc.**
Design: **Ariel Aguilera and Andrea Benyi
  at Pandarosa**
Country: **Australia**

## Platform Artists Group Inc.

Platform is a public art gallery that exhibits works in cabinets situated on the platforms of Melbourne's main train station. It commissioned Pandarosa to design its new logo to coincide with its 10th anniversary. "They asked us to have fun and make a contemporary icon which gave them a new image and would help them move into a new decade as a gallery," explain Aguilera and Benyi. "The idea was to create a logo that could be continuously reinterpreted, from one application to another, by remixing different elements within it." The look and feel came from typography related to railway signal signage and cargo trains, and the shape is an outline of the architectural area where the gallery is located. A custom typeface was created for this logo, which has been applied on signage, the gallery website, invitations, and posters.

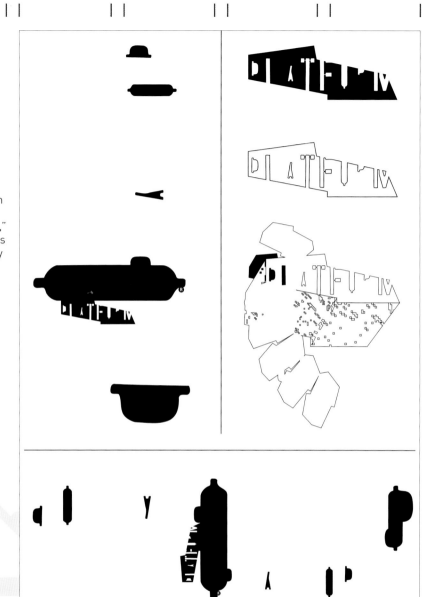

Client: **Create Berlin**
Design: **Martin Christel at Codeluxe**
Country: **Germany**

## Create Berlin

Create Berlin represents Berlin design on an international level. It was founded in 2005/2006 when Berlin was nominated City of Design by UNESCO. The logo was selected at a public competition organized by Create Berlin in which there were 130 competitors. The brief to designers stipulated that the logo should represent Berlin and design from Berlin in its creative variety, and at the same time should serve as a label for both the members of the association and distinguished design from Berlin. Christel's design won. "I created a logo that can be punched manually—it injures, it marks, it makes use of coincidences— but has no particular color," he explains. "Its specific character is caused by the creative processes of others, and in an abstract form it shows the initials of Create Berlin." A special tool was created for hand punching the logo into various media, including letterheads, business cards, and invitations.

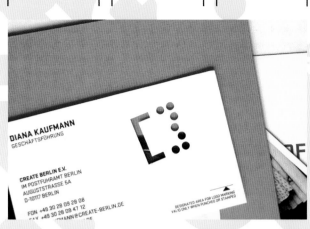

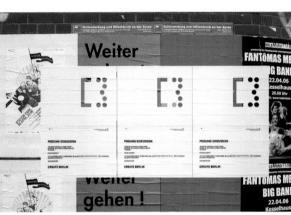

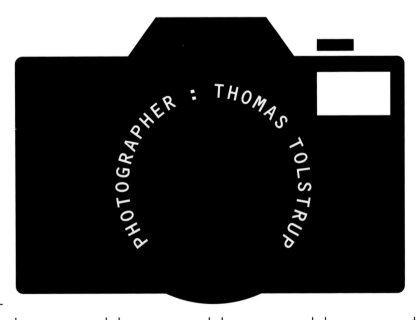

Client: **Thomas Tolstrup**
Design: **Claus Due at Designbolaget**
Country: **Denmark**

## Thomas Tolstrup

Thomas Tolstrup, an award-winning photographer of both people and places, commissioned Due to create his logo. "Tolstrup is originally from the school of journalism—and even now that he works in the field of advertising, the story of his background is important to him," explains Due. "The camera is his tool, and the lens is his way of capturing and telling stories." So the use of the camera image within the logo makes sense. "Naturally we discussed whether it was too banal to show a camera from a photographer, but since we both are fans of clichés, we decided to go with it," he adds. Letter Gothic typeface was used because it is similar to those used on photographers' contact sheets.

Client: **Studio/ Louise Campbell**
Design: **Martin Saunders at BB/Saunders**
Countries: **Denmark/UK**

## Studio/ Louise Campbell

Studio/ Louise Campbell, a Danish furniture design company, asked BB/ Saunders to create its logo. "We got involved in writing the brief with Louise from the start," explains Saunders. "We devised a series of questions, the answers of which formed the structure of the brief. We understood that being sympathetic to her Danish/English heritage was important, but the rigor in Louise's work is at the heart of everything she does—this became the focus for our solution." BB/Saunders wanted to create a logo that didn't pigeonhole Campbell with a style, but would sit comfortably with all the different material the studio produces. It also needed to be beautifully crafted, but extremely robust. The logo used Helvetica Neue 75 and 25, and has been applied to the company's stationery and website. All the stationery employs a white foil block.

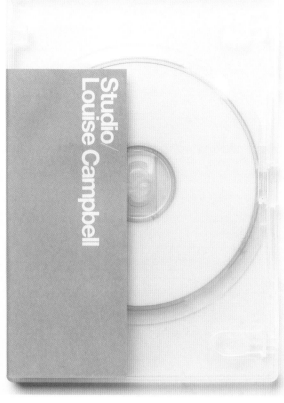

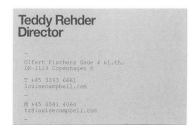

Client: **Standard 8**
Design: **Browns**
Country: **UK**

## Standard 8

Standard 8 specializes in designing and manufacturing 3-D objects—everything from one-off tables to universal exhibition systems. To reflect Standard 8's product and design, its identity is anything but standard. It is made of eight different logos, each made up of eight figure 8s from eight typefaces. Browns' idea was to take an easily recognizable form— the figure eight—and create something interesting and beautiful (finding out only later that the flower-like symbols are called "fleurons"). Each piece of stationery uses a different fleuron. The letterhead is foil blocked with a fluorescent orange foil, the continuation is debossed, and the business cards and compliments cards feature a full set of the logos foil blocked onto the reverse, again in fluorescent orange. The logos are accompanied by a simple wordmark.

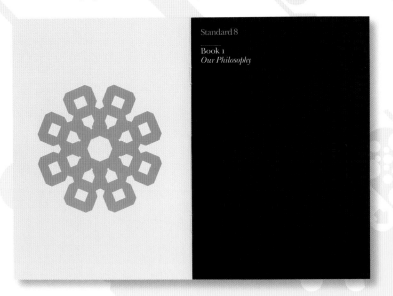

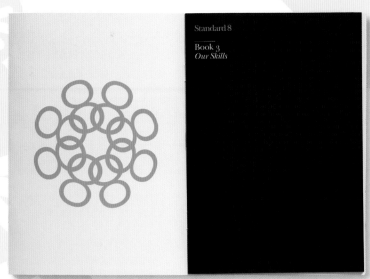

## Ross Imms, A-Side Studio, UK

**What do you think makes a good logo?**
A good logo builds and communicates strong brand values.
It stimulates a response and is created to appeal on a functional,
stylistic, and emotional level. The success of a logo can only
be judged by the response of the target audience.

**Which are your favorite three logos?**
Nike's "swoosh" icon is remarkably versatile. Its simplicity
gives it global appeal and allows it to maintain credibility across
many cultures, subcultures, continents, and classes. A style-
savvy skateboarder will pay a premium for a limited-edition
pair of Dunks on eBay while a studious athlete will wear the
swoosh with pride on the running track. The Nike "swoosh"
forms the backbone of an untouchable lifestyle brand. Guinness
demonstrates seamless integration between product and
brand; this is supported by engaging graphic devices, such as
Brian Boru's Harp, which pay homage to a strong visual heritage.
Its advertising and marketing efforts are consistently cutting
edge and have built a cult following for the drink. Growing up
in the 80s, I was completely immersed in skateboard culture—
the logos and graphics that were imported in the form of
stickers, board graphics, and in magazines were an insight
into American youth culture. Jim Phillips was one of the
pioneers of this graphic movement, creating the visual
identity for Santa Cruz Skateboards. His Speed Wheels
Screaming Hand logo made a deep, lasting impression
the first time I saw it emblazoned on a T-shirt, and it still
brings back memories of hot tarmac and scabby knees.

**What has been your most successfully designed logo?**
Our studio identity remains a firm favorite. It fuses a lower-
and uppercase "A" through an abstract form to create a simple,
versatile identity. It works on-screen and in print effectively.

**When approaching the design of a logo what inspires you?**
First we endeavor to gather a thorough understanding
of the brand. We research the marketplace to establish the
visual tone of potential competitors, then we look at the visual
and conceptual possibilities of the brand—the best ideas often
come from the most obscure sources. When the research
is in place, we embark on an extensive visual brainstorm;
sometimes the letterforms suggest a direction, or the name
that we're working with may dictate the usage of a specific
image. The client will occasionally be involved at this stage,
but usually we will refine the ideas and present a selection
of three strong directions for discussion. The final solution
will be developed from these ideas.

**In some cases there are many places a logo may need
to be applied—how much of a consideration is that when
designing a logo?**
Versatility is a key concern when designing a logo. Most
brands require an on-screen presence that works alongside
their printed materials. Logos may be reproduced in one color
on newsprint and full color on huge billboards. The challenge is
to create a logo and supporting brand elements that accommodate
both ends of the spectrum. We always develop a set of brand
guidelines that dictate how the logo should be used on the
various platforms to ensure continuity.

**What is the most important job for a logo to do?**
To build and communicate strong brand values.

## Stefan Sagmeister, Sagmeister Inc., USA

**What do you think makes a good logo?**
A good logo sticks in my mind and my mind doesn't mind it sticking there.

**Which are your favorite three logos?**
The penguin for Penguin books. I don't remember who designed it. I like it because it's warm, smart, amicable, everywhere, able to replace the word "Penguin," and, most of all, actually stands for good content. I also like Köln, Kunsthochschule für Medien (Academy of Media Arts, Cologne) poster designed by Uwe Loesch in 1990. I love the way that square is closed off on two sides and bleeds into the public realm on the two other edges. It's a glorious spin on Malevitch and more modern than the modernists. Then 24 Corn Cure, designed in 1891, anonymous, no comment necessary.

**What has been your most successfully designed logo?**
Casa da Música, the music center built by Rem Koolhaas in Porto (see page 123). We developed a system where this recognizable, unique, modern form transforms itself like a chameleon from application to application—it changes from medium to medium where the physical building itself is the ultimate (very high-res) rendering in a long line of logos. Our goal was to show the many different kinds of music performed in one house. Depending on the music it is filled with, the house changes its character and works, dice-like, by displaying different views and facets of music.

**When approaching the design of a logo what inspires you?**
That depends completely on the client. For Casa da Música I traveled to Porto, looked at the building, interviewed the president, the musical director, and the director of the orchestra, looked around Porto, enjoyed a couple of performances, studied the program, checked out the competition, and, in short, carried out all the necessary standard research.

**In some cases there are many places a logo may need to be applied—how much of a consideration is that when designing a logo?**
It will inform the design right from the start. When I was in art school, the rule was that any logo needed to be printable in one color on the facet of a pencil, which is somewhat disingenuous because most logos will never wind up there, and could in fact incorporate complexity.

**What is the most important job for a logo to do?**
That depends completely on the client. Sometimes it has to work as a unifier, putting all the various pieces of an organization together. Sometimes it needs to work as a mark of quality, telling a consumer that this has been made and approved by a certain entity. At other times, it will need to be a transformer, showing off the flexibility of a program.

## 05

"I think simplicity is one of the key factors of a good logo—the more that can be communicated using the fewest possible elements, the better."

Ben Cave, UK

Charities & Services

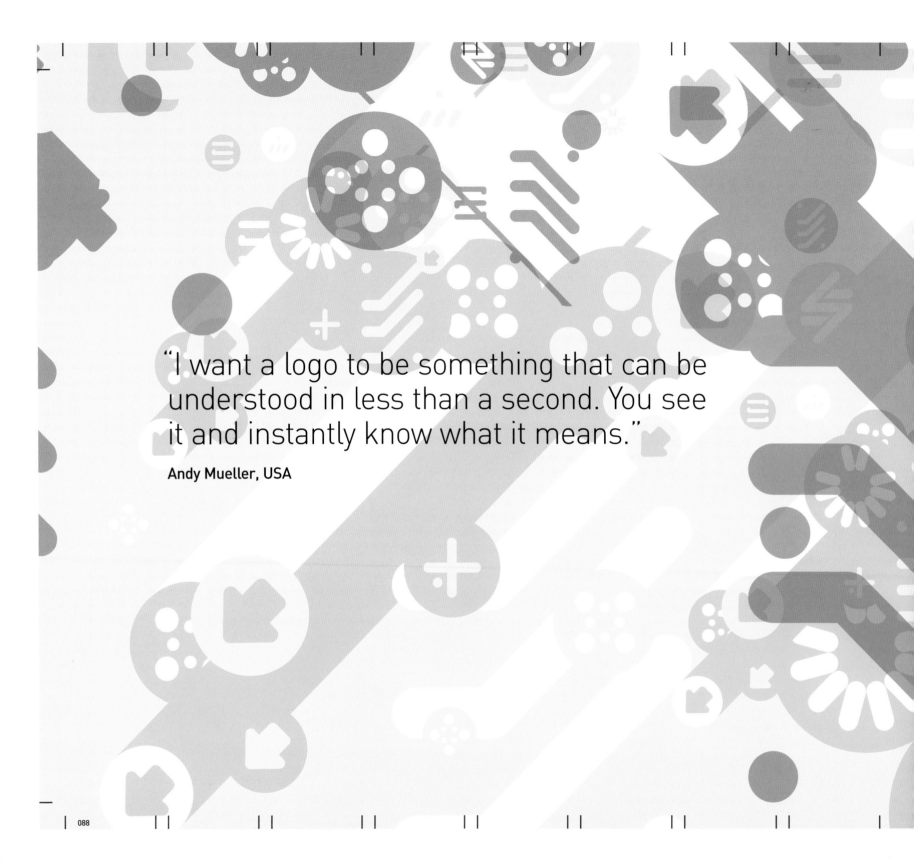

"I want a logo to be something that can be understood in less than a second. You see it and instantly know what it means."

**Andy Mueller, USA**

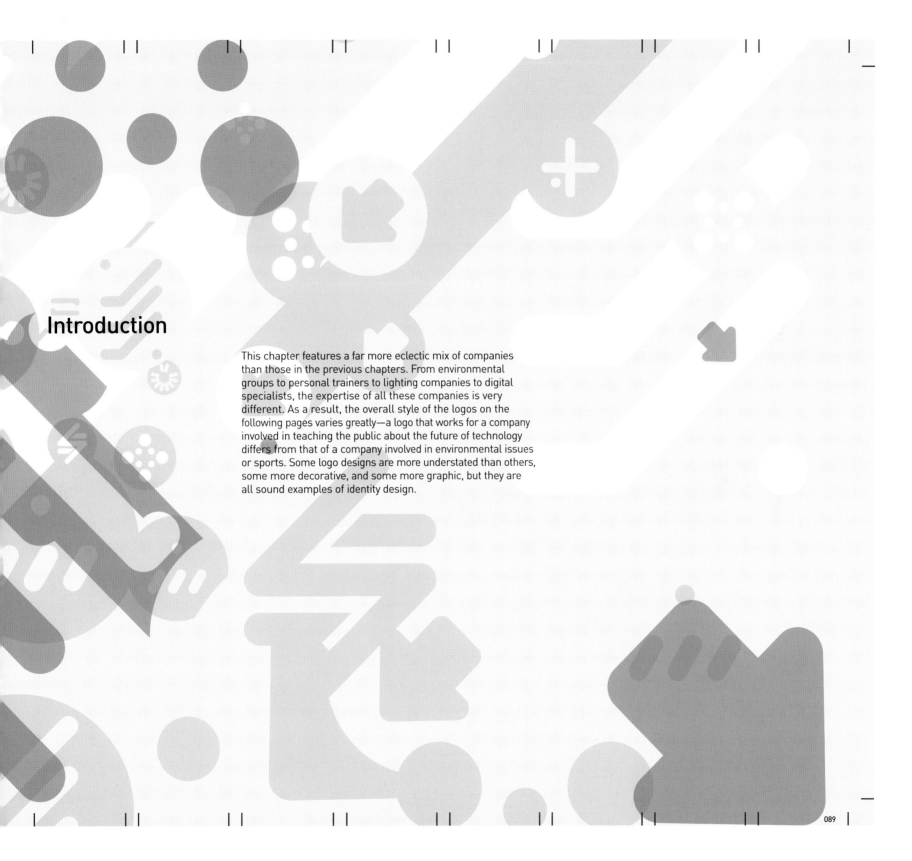

# Introduction

This chapter features a far more eclectic mix of companies than those in the previous chapters. From environmental groups to personal trainers to lighting companies to digital specialists, the expertise of all these companies is very different. As a result, the overall style of the logos on the following pages varies greatly—a logo that works for a company involved in teaching the public about the future of technology differs from that of a company involved in environmental issues or sports. Some logo designs are more understated than others, some more decorative, and some more graphic, but they are all sound examples of identity design.

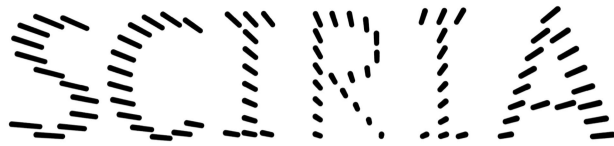

Client: **Sensory Computer Interface Research & Innovation for the Arts (SCIRIA)**
Design: **Christian Küsters at CHK Design**
Country: **UK**

### SCIRIA

SCIRIA challenges and develops the nature and role of the computer interface in the arts. Its practice-informed research leads to the development of multisensory interaction tools for artists and designers within the creative practice. The logo design had to express SCIRIA's academic nature, yet make it accessible and open to the creative practitioners it is firmly connected to. "The idea behind the design was to encapsulate the technological side of the company and do something creative within it," explains Küsters. "Initial ideas and visuals were of 3-D abstract graphical images with which the viewer could interact; we drew on these feelings of touch and technology and translated them into a tangible identity for this forward-looking company." Küsters designed the dot matrix and the logo was applied to the company's stationery and general printed matter.

Client: **Plan8 Konsult**
Design: **Nikolaj Knop at WE RECOMMEND**
Country: **Sweden**

### Plan8

One week Plan8's work might be recommendations on garbage disposal, and the next a plan for cleaner water. So, it needed a logotype to act as a cornerstone for its various business activities rather than reflecting one area of expertise. "We based the logotype around the characteristics of the company's name," explains Knop, "and created a visually strong and dynamic symbol that is durable and allows changes in the business direction of Plan8." The typeface is a modified version of Chalet.

Client: **Fernando Gabeira/Cadu Tavares**
Design: **Alex Nako at Dimaquina**
Country: **Brazil**

## Fernando Gabeira 2006

Dimaquina created this campaign logo for Fernando Gabeira, a Brazilian politician and founder of the national Green Party. Gabeira is a well-recognized character, both for his image and his personality. "Because we've being working with Fernando Gabeira for a long time, the logo shows the openness that he has with us, trusting our aesthetic instincts," explains Nako. "We have Gabeira's iconic face as the main silhouette for the logo—one of the requirements of the brief. The challenge was to represent the modern and dynamic way of thinking the politician has, so we decided to break the silhouette apart, creating a fluid environment inside it." The typeface used for the logo, and the rest of the campaign, was News Gothic. The logo was used on the website, one of the main tools for the campaign, and also on brochures, cars, and T-shirts.

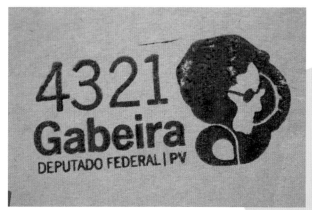

Client: **Wingspan Arts**
Design: **Roanne Adams**
Country: **USA**

## Wingspan Arts

Wingspan Arts is a not-for-profit educational organization that offers art and music programs to children in public schools in New York. It commissioned Adams to redesign its existing logo to enliven the brand, brighten the color palette, and create a strong identity that could stand out against other not-for-profit organizations. As it is based around children, Adams decided to create its logo using children's arts supplies. "The 'butterfly' logo is based on the series of Rorschach-esque prints that I did using finger paints," explains Adams. "After painting, folding, and drying the prints, I chose the painting that looked as close to a butterfly as possible, to represent an animal with a wingspan." The typeface used within the logo is based on ITC American Typewriter, a fun, playful typeface that suits the nature of the Wingspan Arts organization. The logo has been applied to everything including T-shirts, children's film festival posters, and the fundraiser benefit invitations.

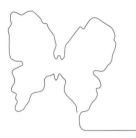

Client: **Silke C. Müller**
Design: **Marc Antosch at**
 **Tilt Design Studio**
Country: **Germany**

## scm

Silke C. Müller, a sports teacher and fitness trainer, commissioned Antosch to create a logo for her business. "The client really had no idea of how her logo should look, so it was totally up to us to come up with some ideas for her," explains Antosch. "Our idea for the logo was just to use the client's initials. I felt the need to make it look 'sporty' in some way and found an illustration in a vintage book on which I based the final illustration." The typeface used is Helvetica Rounded Bold, and the logo has been applied to business cards, envelopes, and business letters.

Client: **Interaction Research Studio,**
 **Goldsmiths, University of London**
Design: **Tim Balaam at Hyperkit**
Country: **UK**

## Material Beliefs

Material Beliefs is a design/engineering research project. Through collaboration, it aims to present engineers' research to the public in an engaging way, and open up debate around the future of technology. Its focus is hybridity and looking at the boundaries between human bodies and materials. Hyperkit was commissioned to design its identity and website. "In response to the subject, we developed a hybrid typeface that would act as the identity for the project," explains Balaam. "This was formed using two existing typefaces: Bodoni Italic represents the human aspect of the project and Foundry Gridnik the more engineered or technical aspect." The logo has been applied on posters, letters, cards, and labels.

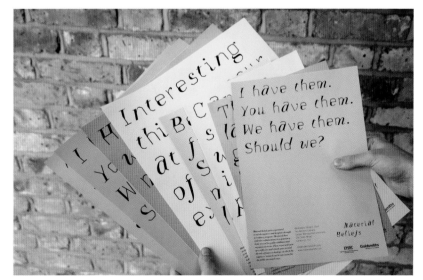

Client: **Save the Children**
Art Direction: **Dan Witchell**
Design: **Proud Creative**
Country: **UK**

## Young People Say

Young People Say is the youth arm of the charity Save the Children. It was set up to get teenagers away from the streets and into other skills on their level—new music, art, and design. "We intentionally avoided the obvious youth clichés such as graffiti/street culture, feeling that they would appear patronizing," explains Witchell. "Instead we focused on creating a straight-forward, bold, and positive marque to reflect the aspirations of the projects. Our aim was to give them a simple identity and let the rest of the graphic language come from the youth team."

Client: **Self-initiated**
Design: **Javin Mo at milkxhake**
Country: **Hong Kong**

## Hug&Kiss

Hug&Kiss is a self-initiated project dedicated to Hong Kong. "It was our self-expression toward the place in which we experienced the outbreak of 'SARS' disease in 2003," explains Mo. "We have created a sweet and lovable identity for our city as well as a new meaning—from Hong Kong to Hug&Kiss. We chose two contrasting and vibrant colors, cyan and magenta, to give a very refreshing energy to the logo. The logo is sweet and can be put together on both sides, to remind people to 'hug and kiss' their friends and family more than ever!"

Client: **St Luke's Lutheran Church**
Design: **David Weik at Studio UKV**
Country: **USA**

## St Luke's Lutheran Church

St Luke's is a 100-year-old inner city church with a contemporary approach to outreach. "For this project the challenge was to create something new for an institution that has been in existence since 1906." There are many symbols used in the Lutheran faith and these provided the starting point for the design. "From here I began to draw inspiration from the actual teachings of the faith," adds Weik. "There were two things I kept coming back to, one being the belief in the Holy Trinity and the other the use of the circle to represent eternal life. By taking three circles and having them abstractly intersecting, I combined the two ideas into one logo." There is also a third symbol formed in the negative space of the mark—an abstracted cross can be seen at the intersection of the three shapes. The simplified shapes and earthy tones represent the church's grass roots, straightforward approach to outreach in the community.

Client: **Direct/Metro Imaging Group**
Design: **Ben Cave and Paul Jenkins**
    **at Ranch**
Country: **UK**

## Direct

Direct is a large lighting- and camera-rental company. "The main requirement of the logo was to place more emphasis on the key services that Direct offers," explains Cave. "Before the rebrand, the company was called Direct Lighting; this did not reflect that it offers a huge range of camera equipment for rental and consumables, in addition to the lighting-rental service. So, these three services needed to be given more prominence. The logo also had to be very flexible, as it was to be applied to a great number of different items." The logo uses a simple, but strong typographical approach to the problem of representing Direct's services. To keep the logo unit flexible, Cave and Jenkins devised three treatments that could be applied to different items, while still retaining a strong brand. Another key benefit of the typographical design was that other words could be substituted into the logo. For Direct's change-of-premises leaflet the logo was altered to read "direct, move, change, relocate." The logo has been applied to many items including stationery, equipment stickers, uniforms, vans, and signage. The typeface is Helvetica Neue.

direct lighting
cameras
consumables

Client: **Northamptonshire County Council**
Design: **Dan Smith at Engine Creative**
Country: **UK**

## Greenscape

This logo was designed for the River Nene Regional Park (RNRP) initiative, a unique, forward-thinking developmental network of environmental, sport, and cultural projects. "Our initial research into the project name was based on creating an umbrella term under which a range of projects could fall," explains Smith. "As with the concept as a whole, we felt that the name needed to be informative, strong, and inspirational. We finally decided on the name 'Greenscape' as it alludes to both the rolling green hills in the area and the village greens, as well as green in terms of being environmentally aware." The illustrative nature of the subsequent logo ties in with the free nature of the initiative and has the ability to utilize various nature-related elements. The illustration is organic and has positive movement, but is underpinned by the strength of the "G," which forms the base from which all of the elements emanate. This is also symbolic of the initiative as a whole—a centrally run venture from which several projects evolve. The flora and fauna were hand-drawn and vectorized for the logo and, to give the intricacy of the illustrative icon strength, Futura Extra Black typeface was used.

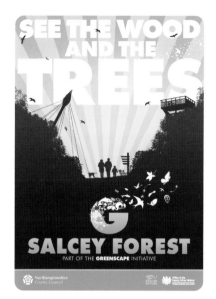

Client: **Take A Risk Foundation**
Design: **karlssonwilker inc.**
Country: **USA**

## Take A Risk Foundation

Take A Risk Foundation provides financial support to risk-takers from all areas of life, including business, science, and the arts. The main idea behind its logo design is a play on man's ancient dream to fly. It is a good example of a simple logo that pairs illustration with text (which is set in Gotham typeface).

Client: **Crofty Consultancy**
Design: **Ross Imms at A-Side Studio**
Country: **UK**

## Crofty Consultancy

Crofty Consultancy, a mining consultancy firm, is one of many businesses within the Wheal Jane Group. Its brief to A-Side Studio was to completely redesign its identity and branding. "The client wanted a fresh, new perspective on their brand to tie in with a business launch, including a revamped office and laboratories," Imms explains. "The identity had to reflect their environmental qualities and maintain their integrity. Their new literature had to be very user-friendly, clear, and concise. For the design of this logo we initially looked at the periodic table, and the use of the initials 'CR' evolved from this. These initials would also be used for other companies within the Group." The imagery within the CR represents elements and soil particles involved in the company's testing.

Old Mine Offices, Wheal Jane, Baldhu, Truro, Cornwall TR3 6EE
t +44 (0)1872 562004 / 5 / 8  f +44 (0)1872 562000  enquiries@wheal-jane.co.uk  www.croftyconsultancy.co.uk

Crofty Consultancy a division of Wheal Jane Services Ltd
Registered office: Wheal Jane Service Ltd, Old Mine Offices, Wheal Jane, Baldhu, Truro, Cornwall TR3 6EE
Registered in England no. 4037548 VAT no. 760 4129 48

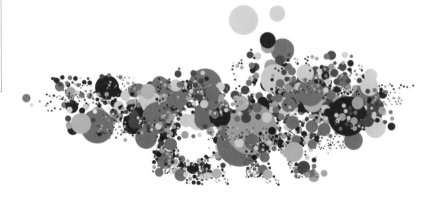

Client: **Push**
Design: **Martin Saunders at BB/Saunders**
Country: **UK**

## Push

Push is a printer with a client base
of predominantly top design agencies.
It wanted to signify its move of premises
and large-scale investment in new
equipment with a new visual identity,
providing a platform for developing the
business further. "We wrote the brief with
the client through several consultations,"
explains Saunders. "There were no
parameters laid down, but the main
objective was to try to personify the key
principles we had agreed on; simplicity
and clarity in the way Push works. This
became the focus for the solution."
The logo is a visual expression of this;
it is a solid and robust mark, distinct and
recognizable. The logo has been applied
to a full range of stationery, sample boxes,
a website, T-shirts, signage, CDs and CD
packaging, packing tape, and coasters.

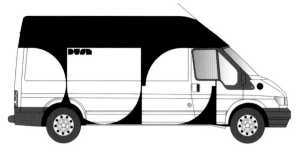

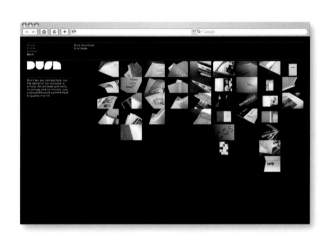

Client: **Green Union**
Design: **Linda Lundin and Nina Nägel**
      **at Park Studio**
Country: **UK**

## Green Union

Green Union supplies information to people
wishing to source, purchase, and utilize
fairly traded, locally produced, and organic
products, food, services, and resources
for weddings and celebrations. "We wanted
to create a logo that reflected an ethical,
friendly, and ecological premise while
being stylish, dynamic, and contemporary,"
explain Lundin and Nägel. "So, we fused
a sans serif with a spring from a serif
to symbolize living nature." The logo has
been used on the company's website
and stationery, which was printed with
vegetable inks on recycled paper.

## Ben Cave, Ranch, UK

**What do you think makes a good logo?**
I think simplicity is one of the key factors of a good logo—the more that can be communicated using the fewest possible elements, the better. This helps in terms of the logo's legibility, and makes it easy to identify. Originality is also important, as a logo needs to be unique to the organization. Ultimately, a good logo is one that successfully projects the desired messages of the organization it represents.

**Which are your favorite three logos?**
The logo for the National Basketball Association [US], designed by Alan Siegel, is a logo that I became very attached to when I was a basketball-obsessed youngster. I used to draw it over and over again. I love its simplicity and the expressive silhouette of the figure. Quite a recent identity that I think works very well is for the Frieze Art Fair, designed by Graphic Thought Facility. I like the blocky arrangement of type, and how the framing device from the logo is also used to frame images and other information that appear alongside. It is a strong and complete identity. The Victoria & Albert Museum logo, designed by Alan Fletcher, is a very popular and well-known logo. It is so simple and concise, while also being elegant and just totally right for the museum. You can't imagine them ever needing to replace it.

**What has been your most successfully designed logo?**
From the logos that Ranch has produced, I would have to choose the "Bollocks to Poverty" campaign logo designed for ActionAid, though I did not have a hand in the creation of this one. Maybe the provocative language helps, but the treatment really captures the spirit of the campaign. It is very punky and almost undesigned. The rough, irreverent aesthetic has become quite iconic and developed a life of its own, appearing everywhere, from tattoos to T-shirts. It is still going strong.

**When approaching the design of a logo what inspires you?**
The best place to start is with general research, and with gathering possible ideas relevant to the client and the field they work in. Then I think it comes down to experimenting with the various elements, such as different typefaces, forms, and arrangements, looking for a hook that works and an idea that can be developed further.

**In some cases there are many places a logo may need to be applied—how much of a consideration is that when designing a logo?**
Considering the various environments in which a logo needs to work is an important part of the design process, although this can vary depending on the nature of the job. It can be hard to predict where a logo will be applied, so a robust, but flexible design is key.

**What is the most important job for a logo?**
To lend a coherent and instantly recognizable voice to a brand.

## Andy Mueller, Ohio Girl, USA

**What do you think makes a good logo?**
There are several things that make a logo good, but, to me, the most important thing is that it has to be simple. I always try to keep it as basic as possible. I want it to be something that can be understood in less than a second. You see it and instantly know what it means. Another reason to keep it simple is so that it can be printed smaller than a dime and as large as a billboard. I always consider this when working on logos. I also think that logos must be able to work in one color—in black and white, without gradients or any values of gray. I've come across a few multicolor logos and I don't like those. I'm still wondering why the UPS traded in the Paul Rand logo for its new brown-and-yellow one with gradients.

**Which are your favorite three logos?**
Anything by Paul Rand is genius so I'm going with three by him. UPS. Classic and simple; the bow detail is amazing without being disruptive. I like how it tells a story of how they will take care, protect your package, and do it with class. They were so silly to redesign that. NeXT Computers. Simple, but clearly shows how this computer was thinking outside the box. It has a futuristic vibe without using trendy typography. ABC. This must be the simplest logo ever made and for that reason I love it. I also want to mention that Saul Bass is amazing as well—his Minolta, United Airlines, and United Way logos are some of my favorites.

**What has been your most successfully designed logo?**
The corporate logo I did for Lakai Limited Footwear is probably my most successful because it's simple, modular, and effective. I like how the "icon" shape on the top of the logo can be removed from the wordmark part of the logo. That icon, called the "flare," can be used on its own and is instantly recognizable as "Lakai Footwear." This logo has been used around the world for about eight years already—on soft goods, shoes, shoeboxes, magazine advertising, online, and everything that's related to Lakai.

**When approaching the design of a logo what inspires you?**
I start by trying to think about the brand and what the brand needs. I like to make sure that I understand the spirit of the brand—that's really the most important thing. Once I know that, then I usually have a good "mental" starting point. My next step is all about the sketchbook. I doodle and doodle and see what comes out. I typically try to develop both wordmark-based logos that say the company's name, and icon-based logos that are more abstract, that "mean" the company without spelling it. I can quickly tell which direction feels best, and go from there.

**In some cases there are many places a logo may need to be applied—how much of a consideration is that when designing a logo?**
I think it's a huge consideration and every logo needs to take this into account. An effective logo must be reproducible in one color, very small and extremely large. So many of my clients are now based in apparel, I have to make sure that logos can not only be printed on a printing press, but also embroidered, stamped, and applied to fabrics in other ways.

**What is the most important job for a logo?**
It has to be the brand.

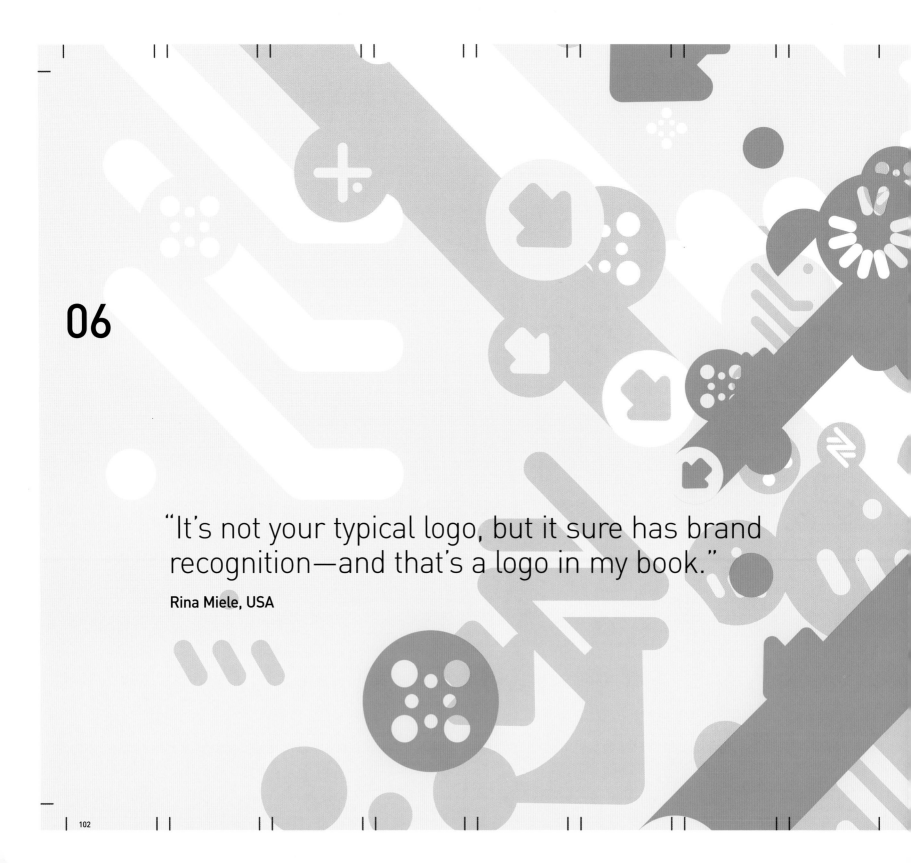

06

"It's not your typical logo, but it sure has brand recognition—and that's a logo in my book."

**Rina Miele, USA**

Music

"A good logo should always try to be different, innovative, and communicate the values of its owner."

**Paul Reardon, UK**

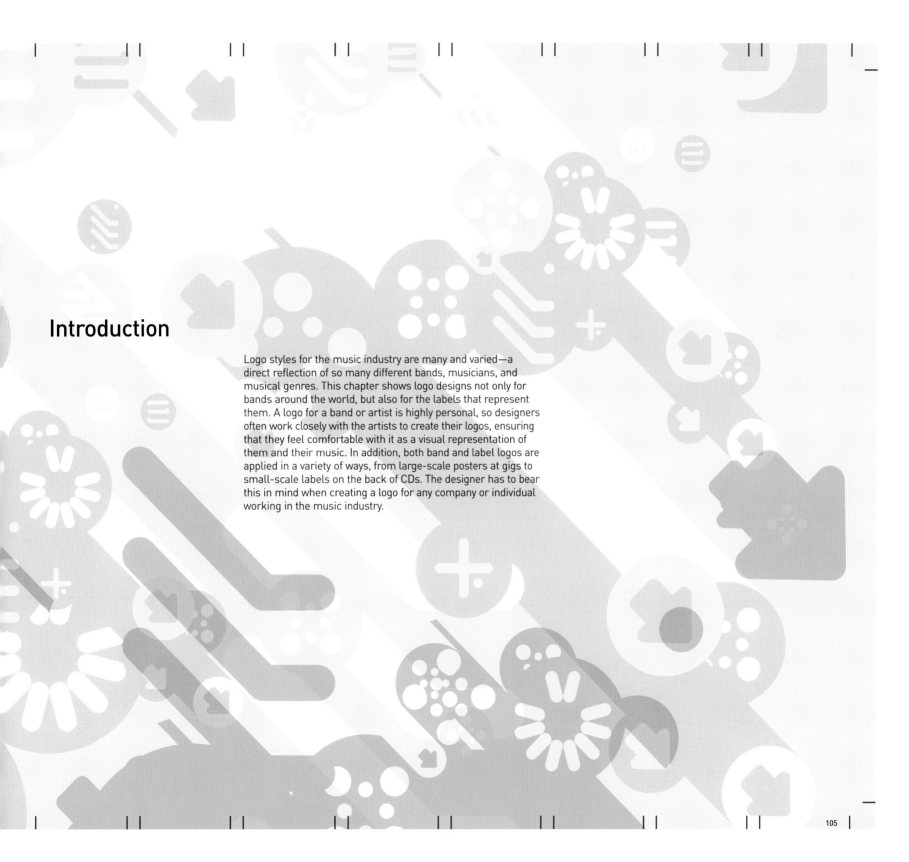

# Introduction

Logo styles for the music industry are many and varied—a direct reflection of so many different bands, musicians, and musical genres. This chapter shows logo designs not only for bands around the world, but also for the labels that represent them. A logo for a band or artist is highly personal, so designers often work closely with the artists to create their logos, ensuring that they feel comfortable with it as a visual representation of them and their music. In addition, both band and label logos are applied in a variety of ways, from large-scale posters at gigs to small-scale labels on the back of CDs. The designer has to bear this in mind when creating a logo for any company or individual working in the music industry.

Client: **Butterfingers**
Design: **Rilla Alexander at Rinzen**
Country: **Germany**

## Butterfingers

Butterfingers, an independent band, commissioned Rinzen to create its logo. "There was no specific direction from the client," explains Alexander. "However, it was clear that the logo needed to be interesting and recognizable, and usable across CDs, posters, and merchandising." The result is a logo that was partially dictated by the prohibitive length of the word "Butterfingers." With so many letters, no sizable pictorial elements could be incorporated without rendering the logo too unwieldy or unclear, so the lettering style needed to carry the

personality of the piece. The band's creative approach references and blends a variety of styles, often irreverent in nature. To reflect this, the styling of the letterforms in the logo avoids any particular genre identification, blending an orderly geometric base with playful flourishes so that the overall look is fluid, bold, and confident. It has been used for advertising and merchandising campaigns, and on CDs and posters.

Client: **Mandoza Family**
Design: **Marc Antosch at Tilt Design Studio**
Country: **Germany**

## Mandoza Family

Mandoza Family plays a mix of 1960s soul and rock 'n' roll music. "There was no concrete briefing; we could do what we wanted," explains Antosch. "The band only asked for a logo that represents the music they play in some way. The idea was to use a clean typeface in combination with some vector illustrations, and in the end the logo has a 'natural' touch." The typeface used was ITC Avant Garde.

# SOME WATER AND SUN

Client: **John Hughes/Hefty Records**
Design: **Jonas Banker at BankerWessel**
Country: **Sweden**

## Some Water and Sun

BankerWessel created this logo for the release of electronic music band Some Water and Sun's first CD/LP, <u>All My Friends Have to Go</u>. The brief was simply, "surprise us." BankerWessel based the logo on the typeface it had created for text featured on the band's CD/LP. "We made a typeface that would work with the pictures on the cover of the CD," explains Banker, "and then used it to create the logo." The result is this cut-out lettering style logo, featuring that typeface.

Client: **Tooth & Nail Records**
Design: **Ryan Clark**
Country: **USA**

## The Lonely Hearts

The Lonely Hearts is an alternative country band and Clark's goal for the logo was to capture its sound by harking back to the days of classic rock and blues. He drew inspiration from bands of the 1960s and 1970s, and used organic lines and stylized details to capture the band's Southern roots and classic sound. Clark created a custom typeface for the logo, but took "the" from an existing Émigré typeface called Brothers.

Client: **The Ark**
Design: **Richard Tillblad at Zion Graphics**
Country: **Sweden**

## The Ark

Zion Graphics designed this logo for Swedish glam rock group The Ark for its tour and album release. This logo was adapted from the logo that Zion Graphics designed for the band's previous release, <u>State Of The Ark</u>. "Because all the artwork for The Ark is inspired by Art Deco, it was natural that the logo be inspired by that era as well. At the same time, it was important that it felt contemporary," explains Tillblad. "This logo was inspired by the typography on an Italian Art Deco poster, which I then hand-drew. The earlier logo we made for The Ark used two different colors, but this new version is made with solid and lined graphics for easier use in different media." The logo was applied to record sleeves, ads, bags, stickers, T-shirts, and videos, and used animated on tour stages. It has also been used gold and silver foiled on limited-edition sleeves.

# ElektronS

**Client:** Elektrons/Wall of Sound
**Design:** Patrick Duffy at No Days Off
**Country:** UK

## Elektrons

Elektrons is a musical project from the Unabombers, founders of the UK's Northern clubbing institution Electric Chair. It commissioned No Days Off to create its logo, giving the brief for it to be "modern psychedelia." "Taking this as inspiration, we investigated elements of psychedelic typography—flowing, swirling lines, fluid shapes—and brought them into the present, giving the identity a clean, modern feeling," explains Duffy. "We designed two versions of the logo— one just as linework and one with a thick border. This was intended to function as a 'sticker' on the sleeve artwork, so that the logo would stand out easily, but still appear as part of the overall collage." The logo is intended to be flexible: it can appear smooth and clean, roughed up and photocopied, scribbled, or with a neon effect, depending on its application across promos, T-shirts, commercial releases, and stickers.

Client: **Tom Liwa**
Design: **Stefan Claudius**
Country: **Germany**

## Ludwig

Tom Liwa, a musician who started his own record company, commissioned Claudius to design his logo. "The funniest thing about this logo is that Liwa called me and dictated the briefing on my answering machine," explains Claudius. "The machine has really poor sound quality and when I was listening to his message I thought I heard him saying, 'Do something with a raven,' but he had actually said 'border'—it sounds similar in German." As a result, Claudius created this logo, which features an image of a raven. "We both had a good laugh about it afterwards, and Liwa loved the logo anyway." The logo is also intentionally bold, plain, and simple because record company logos often appear in very small sizes on the backs of CDs. Claudius used one of his own fonts, CA Emeralda™.

Client: **Dez Mona**
Design: **Emmi Salonen at Emmi**
Countries: **Belgium/UK**

## Dez Mona

Belgium-based Dez Mona is a musical duo featuring double bass player Nicolas Rombouts and vocalist Gregory Frateur. Its sound could be described as a mixture of jazz, drama, experimental, and spiritual, with some of its album tracks having quite dark overtones. It commissioned Emmi to create a logo for use on its releases, posters, and website. "For the design of the logo, I was inspired mainly by the music, and the dark feel that some of their songs have," explains Salonen. "They are quite an experimental duo and I wanted the logo to reflect that."

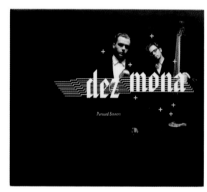

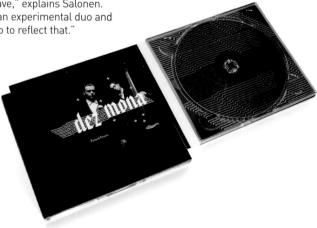

Client: **Sellwell Records**
Design: **Clemens Baldermann**
    at **Purple Haze Studio**
Country: **Germany**

## Forbidden Fruit (parts 1 and 2)

Sellwell Records is a small record label specializing in producing vinyl for DJs and producers. "The idea behind the title-type designs and logos was to create bold, individual typographies in conjunction with the illustrations of the cover artworks, in turn creating a unique and strong visibility that also underlines the limited-edition character of the vinyl records series," explains Baldermann. Inspiration for the design came from old-fashioned labels, nameplates, and iconic religious images. All in-house custom-made typefaces were used. Both of these sleeve designs received a Certificate of Typographic Excellence award from the Type Directors Club, New York.

Client: **GeeJam Studios**
Design: **David Calderley**
at **GraphicTherapy**
Countries: **Jamaica/USA**

## Forward Recordings

Forward Recordings is a recording, artist management, and artist development company, as well as a recording studio and part of GeeJam Studios. It asked Calderley to create its identity with the brief for it to be "urban," yet clean and contemporary, and, importantly, to utilize classic colors of Jamaica. "They wanted a logo that could work in all manner of print without losing impact," explains Calderley. "We started off with a hard slab sans serif, then took a series of images from walls with graffiti and Jamaican urban folk art, which we then split into the type, randomly breaking it up." The font used began its life as Gridnik.

Client: **Alain Emile**
Design: **Rina Miele at Honey Design**
Country: **USA**

## Doux Electronique

Doux Electronique is the alias of New York–based sound designer/producer/ composer Alain Emile who created it for his music ventures. A loose interpretation of the name would be "Soft Electronic." Emile commissioned Miele to create an identity for his alias. The two discussed making it look sexy and fun, but Emile gave Miele full creative freedom. "The main idea for the identity was essence," explains Miele. "I wanted to capture that intrinsic quality of what Doux was in a single glance. I felt it needed to be modern, energetic, and 'soft' while maintaining that sexy edge." The logo uses custom-made and hand-drawn letters by Miele.

Client: **Hookah Brown**
Design: **David Calderley**
 at **GraphicTherapy**
Country: **USA**

## Hookah Brown

Hookah Brown is the side project of Rich Robinson from The Black Crowes. Calderley's brief was to create something a bit "hazy" and early 1970s–inspired. "We presented many different ideas for this project," explains Calderley. "The final choice was a combination of two of those ideas and features Art Nouveau elements together with some hand-drawn pieces and an old photo-lettering font from a type-specimen book from the 70s." The logo has been applied to CDs, T-shirts, and posters.

Client: **Kanister Records**
Design: **André Nossek at Via Grafik**
Country: **Germany**

## 1+1=11

This logo was designed for the remix release of one of 1+1=11's maxi singles. The cover was made up of yellow and green earth tape so it seemed natural for Via Grafik to continue this theme in the logo. "The idea was to use tape as type," explains Nossek. "Because the band plays electronic music, we decided to use this green and yellow tape, which is normally used to isolate electronic cables."

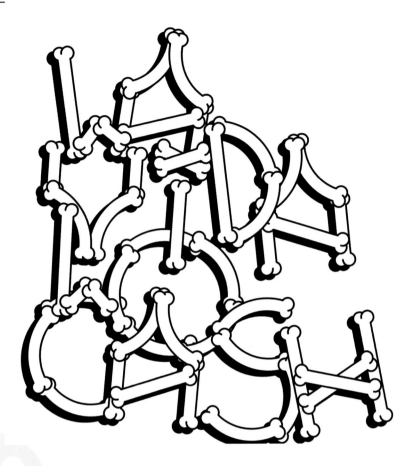

Client: **La Vida Locash**
Design: **Micke Thorsby at PMKFA**
Countries: **Japan/Sweden**

### La Vida Locash
La Vida Locash is an independent record label famed for launching the careers of Lo-Fi-Fnk and more recently Kocky. "I wanted to create a cartoon-style lettering for the label," he explains. "I didn't want to use actual characters for the logo; I wanted it to look like Mickey Mouse's skeleton in a pile." The logo has been used on records, flyers, posters, and the label's website.

Client: **We the People Records**
Design: **Stefan Claudius**
Countries: **Germany/USA**

### Firescape
Claudius was commissioned to design the logo for Firescape's album launch. "They sent us their MySpace link, told us to listen to the music, and then make a design," explains Claudius. "We wanted it to be rough and plain, yet a bit arty, I guess like the music that the band played." The result is a logotype based on Claudius' own CA Coronado.

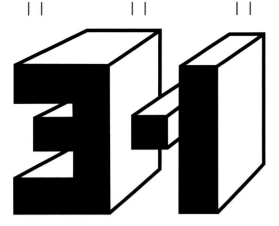

**Client: 3-1**
Design: **Ivo Schmetz at 310k**
Country: **The Netherlands**

### 3-1

3-1, an electro band, is known for its live shows combining video and music. The idea behind this logo design is a simple 3-D effect. "At first the logo was hand-drawn, as are many of the things created for this band," explains Schmetz, "but we decided to redraw the logo in Illustrator so it could be used in more ways." The logo has been applied to stickers, stamps, CD prints, T-shirts, buttons, and also on record covers.

Client: **The Williams**
Design: **Christian Albriktsen**
Country: **Norway**

### The Williams

In his brief for this logo, "I received a bunch of pictures of old movie posters reflecting the style of logo the band was after," explains Albriktsen. "It was also important to keep it simple." His idea for the logo was sparked by a photograph of the band. With the images of the movie posters in his head, he chose to give the logo an American Western feel, which he felt complemented the band's music. The typeface used is Utopia Italic, modified to give the logo a unique identity.

Client: **Studio 5610**
Design: **one-two.org**
Country: **Switzerland**

## Studio 5610

Studio 5610, a small record label founded in 2006 by Martin Muntwyler, focuses on young and upcoming bands. It worked closely with one-two.org to develop the concept for this logo, including the company name (5610 is the studio's postcode) and the visual (the sloth is one of its favorite animals). The typeface selected was Lineto's Akkurat Bold. The logo has been applied to various media including business cards, T-shirts, matches, and fliers.

# Studio 5610

Client: **Felt Music**
Design: **Adam Pointer**
Country: **UK**

## Felt Music

Felt Music works closely with the
advertising industry, dealing with
music production, creative searches,
license negotiation, sound design, and
composition. "The design evolved from
an earlier commission to design the cover
for its annual summer sampler entitled
<u>Bloom</u>," explains Pointer. "The brief for
this was simply to create something that
was evocative of summer freshness
and creation, with a reference to the
music. Felt was really positive about the
artwork and idea, and keen to see how it
could be transformed into an image to
become a new identity for the company,
which is what I did." The resultant logo
reflects and demonstrates the balance
between its creativity and functionality.
Lubalin Graph typeface was used for the
logo, which was applied on a set of library
CDs representing the different musical
genres offered by Felt, a promotional
T-shirt, and its office window stickers.

Client: **Play It By Ear**
Design: **Jody Hudson-Powell and**
**Luke Powell at Hudson-Powell**
Country: **UK**

## Play It By Ear

Play It By Ear is a biweekly live music night. It wanted a unique symbol that could be easily recognized in magazines and on fliers. "When we started work on the Play It By Ear logo, we knew that our involvement in the logo would stop after the logo's creation and initial flier," explain Powell and Hudson-Powell. "With this as a starting point, we decided that the logo should stand separate from any design style or wordmark, and be used like a sticker, literally placed anyhow over the top of any other design." The result is a logo that borrows from the language of modern pictograms. While the symbol is immediately recognizable as an ear, it is also hard not to notice a character with a very broad smile when turned 180°.

Client: **HATTLER**
Design: **Jan Wilker at karlssonwilker inc.**
Country: **USA**

## flying hattler

HATTLER, an electronic band hailing from Germany, asked karlssonwilker inc. to create a logo for the release of its album Bass Cuts. The idea for the logo was simple, as Wilker explains. "We asked Mr. Hattler to do an action photo shoot for us, and the 'flying hattler' that came out of that shoot struck a chord with us, so we used it as the logo." The simple, yet memorable logo has been used on all materials for the album and its release.

Client: **Widespread Panic**
Design: **Chris Bilheimer**
Illustration: **Chris Bilheimer**
Country: **USA**

## Widespread Panic 1

Bilheimer is often commissioned to design posters for Widespread Panic when it tours, and for each poster he designs a new logo. He created this logo typeface using Freehand and ink applied together with imagery using a seven-color silkscreen print. "The entire piece was inspired by watercolor paintings I'd seen at a gallery in Barcelona," he explains. "I was drawn to the look of different colors bleeding into one another, and tried to get a similar effect with the silkscreen printing of this poster."

Client: **Widespread Panic**
Design: **Chris Bilheimer**
Illustration: **Chris Bilheimer**
Country: **USA**

## Widespread Panic 2

The poster shown here was inspired by the band's environmental preservation. Bilheimer created the illustration by laying wooden matches on a scanner in the shape of the tree and then drawing on the flame-leaves by hand. The title type mimics writing that might have been drawn with a burnt-out match. The limited-edition poster was silkscreen printed in four colors.

Client: **Capô de Fusca**
Design: **Leonardo Eyer at Caótica**
Country: **Brazil**

## Capô de Fusca

Capô de Fusca is an independent rock 'n' roll band. This, the band's first logo, was designed by Eyer for its debut album. There was no briefing; instead, Eyer went to the band's recording sessions, listened to its music, and started from there. Inspired by this, and the band's name (Fusca is the Volkswagen Beetle in Brazil and Capô the word for the front hood of a car, but Capô de Fusca has other meanings, mainly related to sex), Eyer created its logo and CD artwork. The alternative meanings of Capô de Fusca were incorporated in the CD artwork, but for the logo itself he used only the car. The illustration in the logo is of the band's first car, which it used when it began touring, and which it still owns. The typeface is ITC Bookman Bold. The logo has been used on the CD, posters, T-shirts, and all promotional pieces.

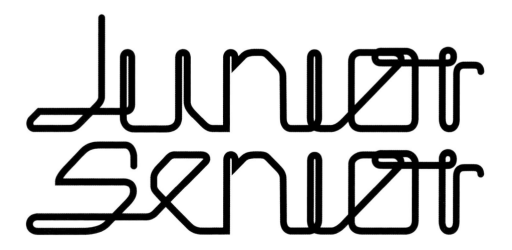

Client: **Crunchy Frog/Junior Senior**
Design: **Micke Thorsby at PMKFA**
Countries: **Denmark/Japan**

## Junior Senior

Junior Senior is signed to record label Crunchy Frog. When Thorsby was commissioned to create the artwork for Junior Senior's first album, he also developed a logo for the band, and has since created all their graphic material. "The idea was to make a logotype using a 'digital' handwriting style," explains Thorsby, "so I created a joined typeface from which to create their logotype. It has been applied on T-shirts, CDs, and vinyl albums, as well as EPs and singles."

Client: **Chieko Mori**
Design: **Emmi Salonen at Emmi**
Countries: **Japan/UK**

## Chieko Mori

Emmi created this identity for Japanese artist Chieko Mori, a Koto (a traditional Japanese stringed instrument) player and singer. Chieko had previously released albums, but had not had a strong identity, hence Salonen's appointment to create one. The brief was to show the appreciation of the history associated with the Koto, while maintaining the fresh and even Western approach Mori has to composing. "My solution was to use a pattern created from ancient Japanese drawings, together with modern Western typography and shapes," explains Salonen. "The identity therefore suggests a new approach to Koto playing, and the use of only the colors of the Japanese flag also reflects the traditional origins of the instrument." The imagery within the identity, and combined with the text, consists of old European-style ornaments and outlines of butterflies. The text is Avant Garde.

Client: **Casa da Música**
Art Direction: **Stefan Sagmeister**
Design: **Quentin Walesch and Matthias Ernstberger at Sagmeister Inc.**
Logo Generation: **Ralph Ammer**
Countries: **Portugal/USA**

## Casa da Música

Sagmeister Inc. created this identity for Casa da Música, the music center in Porto designed by Rem Koolhaas. It initially wanted to design an identity without featuring the building, but this proved impossible. "As we studied the structure, we realized that the building itself is a logo," explains Sagmeister. "But we did try to avoid another rendering of a building by developing a system by which its recognizable, unique, form transforms itself from application to application and changes from medium to medium, where the physical building itself is the ultimate rendering in a long line of logos." Its goal was to show the many different kinds of music performed in one house, so, depending on the music, the logo changes its character, working dice-like by displaying different views and facets.

 casa da música

 casa da música

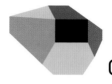 casa da música

 casa da música

 casa da música

Client: **Below Par Records**
Design: **Rilla Alexander at Rinzen**
Countries: **Germany/UK**

## The Scare

For this logo, Rinzen had no initial brief from the band, "other than to create something cool," explains Alexander. The idea was to create a very specific, immediately identifiable "mark" for the band's music and style. "Using inspiration from 1970s stadium band logos, we developed a brand that could work across a huge variety of applications, and be immediately identifiable as the band's product," adds Alexander. "The 'look' evolved naturally from evaluating old stadium band logos—Van Halen and the Electric Light Orchestra—through seeing the band perform live, and having one-on-one meetings with them."

Client: **Milk**
Design: **Base Design**
Country: **USA**

## Milk Salon

Milk is a group of companies involved in fashion, photography, music, and art. This logo was created for a classical music performance series hosted by Milk called Milk Salon. "The logo had to incorporate the existing 'Milk' logo, yet be strong enough as a whole to read as 'Milk Salon,'" explains Base Design. "The idea behind the identity is to update the classic Salon concept. A contrast is always present—between the geometric Milk logo and the classic, elegant script of 'Salon.'" This idea of contrast continues through the applications; the hand-delivered invitations, for example, consisted of classic fresh flowers in red acrylic boxes with silkscreened logo and text. Univers condensed typeface was used for "Milk" and Chopin Script for "Salon." Both typefaces were altered for the logo.

**Client: Form Music**
**Design: Richard Robinson**
**Country: UK**

## Form

Form Music is a music research, composition, licensing, and brand communication company. It provides a variety of creative music solutions and consultancy services across the industries of advertising, TV, film, and new media. "This was a very open brief," Robinson explains, "although we had discussed the importance of it being a classic, clean design that could work across a variety of formats without dating too fast." Form Music offers a more refined response than its competitors and the logo needed to reflect this philosophy. No imagery was used on the mark itself, but the logo works in conjunction with floral patterns from an old fabric sample. The type was custom-made.

**Client: Kate Nash/Fiction**
**Design: Patrick Duffy at No Days Off**
**Country: UK**

## Kate Nash

Kate Nash's songs contain great story-telling elements. No Days Off created this logo, which features on her promos and commercial releases. "We wanted the logo to have a simple, hand-drawn appearance to fit in with the 'home-grown' philosophy that Kate applies to her music and artwork," explains Duffy. "We liked the idea of creating something with a slight storybook aesthetic, without being too cutesy, which again fits in with the music Kate makes: funny, and with a sense of fantasy, but always rooted in reality." The lettering was inspired by a hand-drawn font, which Duffy had seen in the sketchbook of his friend and illustrator Chris Graham, and is a bold typeface with a rough edge to it.

Client: **Arm The Lonely**
Design: **Alexander Egger**
Country: **Austria**

## Arm The Lonely

Arm The Lonely is an independent platform for music including a record label, tour organization, art exhibitions, performances, and literature. Egger's identity for the project was inspired by grain, noise, sequences, cut-ups, and cheap reproduction techniques. The logo appears to be an accidental assemblage of forms, imbuing it with a raw power and subversive potential. It was applied across promo booklets, CDs, posters, and badges. It has been variously stamped, cut out, sprayed, and projected as concert visuals.

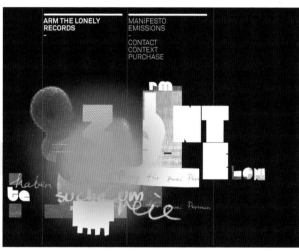

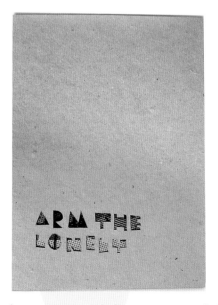

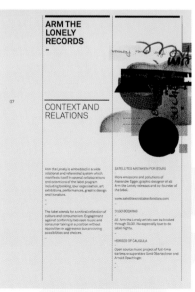

Client: **The Hove Festival**
Design: **Samuel Muir at Neighbour**
Illustration: **Ian Stevenson**
Countries: **Norway/UK**

## The Hove Festival

The Hove Festival is an international music festival held in Norway. It asked Neighbour to create the logo for its launch. The brief was to quickly establish the Hove Festival in the mind-set of young festivalgoers and represent the experience of attending the music festival. "We created the logo as a single organic form that has been ripped apart," explains Muir. "The H and O sit on the top line, while the V and E have pulled away to the second line, leaving a trail of innards splattered across the ground." The concept was to provide a surreal snapshot of all the goings-on at a festival. The logo was hand painted and redrawn by Neighbour; the secondary typeface is Futura. The logo has been applied to all marketing material promoting the festival, including press and television advertising, posters, and website.

Client: **!K7 Records**
Design: **Purple Haze Studio**
Country: **Germany**

## Voom Voom

!K7 Records is renowned as one of the most diverse and influential independent labels for electronic music worldwide, representing artists such as Vroom Vroom, Kruder & Dorfmeister, Herbert, Swayzak, and Funkstörung. "The idea was to create a bold title-type logo for a series of record covers that could contrast the separate vinyls not only via the different cover artworks, but also on the type level. Inspiration for the designs came from 1970s and 1980s cover art-works, airbrush, plastic, gloss, cables, geometric figures, and paint brush."

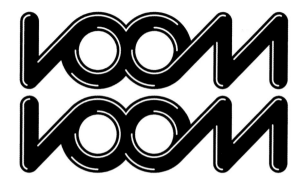

Client: **Earth Records**
Design: **Paul Reardon at Peter & Paul**
Country: **UK**

## The Lovers

Peter & Paul designed this logo for French band The Lovers, aka Fred and Marion. It began as something The Lovers could use on 12in promos, and was designed simply as a reflection of their personalities. "At heart Fred and Marion are old-fashioned romantics, so we decided to create the logo as a modern take on an old-fashioned crest," explains Reardon. "The heads of Fred and Marion form the centerpiece, while ornate decorative swirls spill out to the edges. On closer inspection these are actually sperm." The images of the couple were taken from photographs and all typography was hand-drawn. The logo was foil blocked in gold for a 12in vinyl release. For this limited-edition album, a scented pouch was made with the logo embroidered on its front.

## Rina Miele, Honey Design, USA

**What do you think makes a good logo?**
I think there are many different kinds of logos. Some are corporate, illustrative, cultural, or media related, political, nonsensical, or none of the above. There are logos for everything and everyone. What makes a logo "good" is if it succeeds in representing the person or thing for which it was intended. If it makes a "mark" then it achieves its goal.

**Which are your favorite three logos?**
They may seem like obvious choices or textbook answers, but my top two logos are probably the Apple Inc. mark and the Nike logo. My third favorite is the Obey Giant "logo."

The Apple logo we see today is more or less the one that was designed by Rob Janoff in 1976, referred to as the "rainbow apple" for its bands of color. His main design is still used; the shape is nearly identical, but with a monochromatic scheme replacing the colors. The icon does not even need to be accompanied by any additional type—only the mark is used. It hasn't changed much in decades and still feels modern. Instantly identifiable, it is simple, clean, and intelligent—all things you'd associate with the company.

Similarly, the Nike "swoosh" logo hasn't changed much since design student Carolyn Davidson created it in 1971. Since then it has appeared on practically everything from shoes, apparel, labels, posters, billboards, websites, tons of ephemera, and beyond. And each time it is used, it still looks fresh, new, smart, and energetic.

A different kind of logo is the Obey Giant created by Shepard Fairey in 1989. It wasn't a logo at first, but a sticker campaign for Andre the Giant. The icon became so widely known, it progressed to become a "logo" for Shepard Fairey. In this case, the identity somehow came to define itself, rather than being defined by the designer. This is what draws me to it—the surprise. It's not your typical logo, but it sure has brand recognition—and that's a logo in my book.

**What has been your most successfully designed logo?**
To me, if a logo represents what it is supposed to, it is successful. I think the logo I created for myself, the Honey Design logo, has had the most success. It's very simple, clean, sophisticated, and modern. It is strong, and I haven't felt the need to change it. The letterforms are quite nice and they work well. It may seem an obvious solution, but there are many iterations you'd never even consider. That's the beauty in all simple logos—they aren't that simple at all.

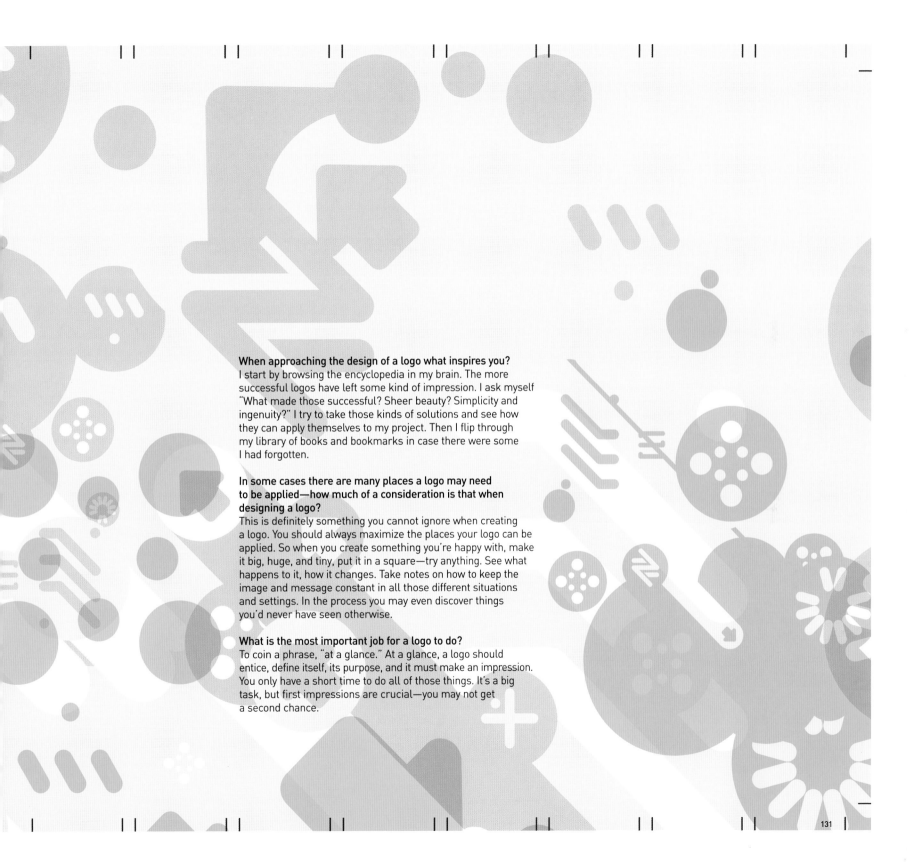

**When approaching the design of a logo what inspires you?**
I start by browsing the encyclopedia in my brain. The more successful logos have left some kind of impression. I ask myself "What made those successful? Sheer beauty? Simplicity and ingenuity?" I try to take those kinds of solutions and see how they can apply themselves to my project. Then I flip through my library of books and bookmarks in case there were some I had forgotten.

**In some cases there are many places a logo may need to be applied—how much of a consideration is that when designing a logo?**
This is definitely something you cannot ignore when creating a logo. You should always maximize the places your logo can be applied. So when you create something you're happy with, make it big, huge, and tiny, put it in a square—try anything. See what happens to it, how it changes. Take notes on how to keep the image and message constant in all those different situations and settings. In the process you may even discover things you'd never have seen otherwise.

**What is the most important job for a logo to do?**
To coin a phrase, "at a glance." At a glance, a logo should entice, define itself, its purpose, and it must make an impression. You only have a short time to do all of those things. It's a big task, but first impressions are crucial—you may not get a second chance.

## Paul Reardon, Peter & Paul, UK

**What do you think makes a good logo?**
I think there are changing attributes to what makes a good logo. If we talk about it within the context of companies and products, it's hard not to mention brand. Historically, you can look back at logo design and appreciate certain logos for having a clever idea or the style of mark making, but as our awareness of design and graphic language becomes more sophisticated, logo design is evermore reliant on the backing of a sound brand. One should inform the other, so the root of this stems from a sound business idea before a designer even puts pen to paper. A good logo should always try to be different, innovative, and communicate the values of its owner.

**Which are your favorite three logos?**
As a student I always loved the PTT postmark designed by Studio Dumbar. Although controlled in its execution, the application of the mark and identity is very free-form and doesn't conform to the dogmatic rules of applying a corporate mark. I also like it because there was lots of last-minute uncertainty from the client over whether the identity was right for them, but time and budget was exhausted, so the project went through unscathed and was a resounding success.

My second choice is the recent identity for the Walker Arts Center. This is not actually a logo, but a design kit of parts consisting of patterns and colors that contain words which can be composed to suit different applications. I like the "paint by numbers" playfulness of the idea. I also like the boldness of an arts organization being brave enough to want to create a very visible graphic language of its own without fear of overwhelming the artists' work and exhibits.

My final choice is very different from the previous two, and a return to a more traditional approach to logo design. It's the logo for the National Interpreting Service recently designed by Browns. Designing a logo for an organization that works in the business of multiple languages is a difficult task. Browns created a simple, singular logo that uses multilingual symbols and characters added to the company name to convey the service of the organization. As an idea it translates universally, without the need to replicate the logo in different languages. It's a great example of solving a seemingly complex problem with a simple, elegant solution.

**What has been your most successful logo?**
It would have to be a logo that Peter and I designed together a few years before we founded Peter & Paul. The client was Manchester Business School [MBS]. MBS is renowned for its unique, freethinking approach to lectures, encouraging open forums for debate and new ideas between teachers and students, known within MBS as the "Manchester Method." The concept for the logo was developed around this freethinking approach. The mark consisted of a purple, hand-drawn square that represented MBS and which its alumni, academics, and students would contribute ideas to in the form of sketched doodles, drawing over, around, and inside the box to turn the object into something new. The more interesting and innovative doodles were selected to be applied to a range of applications from signage to prospectuses. Before this project, the way in which we thought about logo identity work had been very formulaic, but here we saw an opportunity to tear up the corporate manual. It had a profound effect on how we approached identity work from then on.

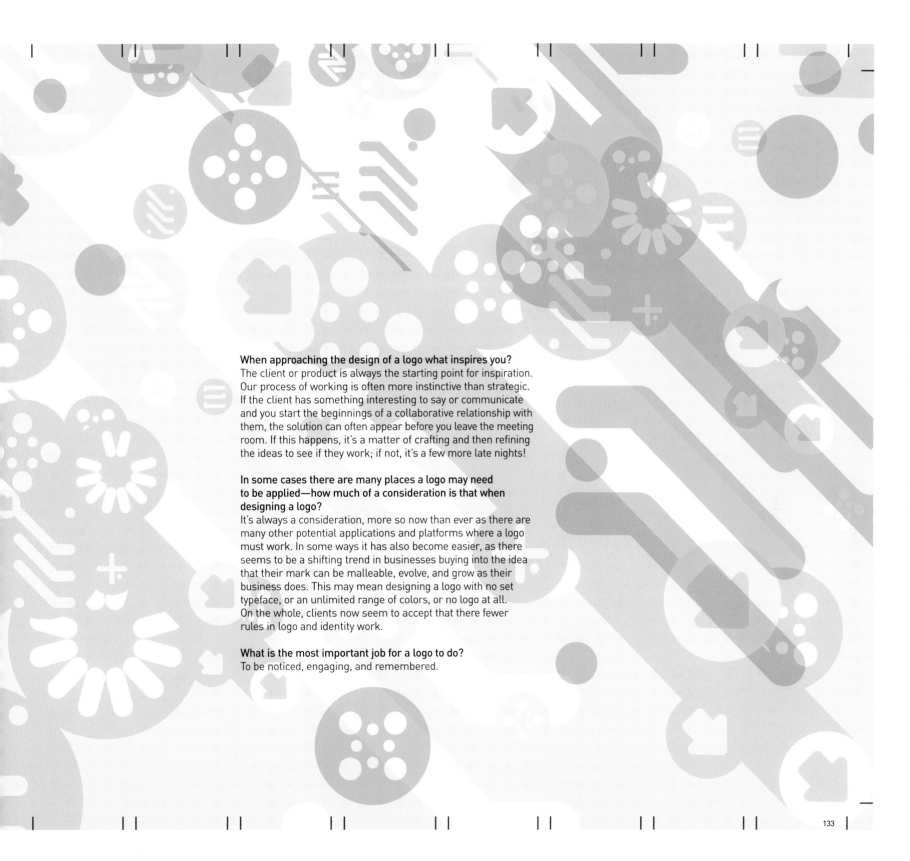

**When approaching the design of a logo what inspires you?**
The client or product is always the starting point for inspiration.
Our process of working is often more instinctive than strategic.
If the client has something interesting to say or communicate
and you start the beginnings of a collaborative relationship with
them, the solution can often appear before you leave the meeting
room. If this happens, it's a matter of crafting and then refining
the ideas to see if they work; if not, it's a few more late nights!

**In some cases there are many places a logo may need
to be applied—how much of a consideration is that when
designing a logo?**
It's always a consideration, more so now than ever as there are
many other potential applications and platforms where a logo
must work. In some ways it has also become easier, as there
seems to be a shifting trend in businesses buying into the idea
that their mark can be malleable, evolve, and grow as their
business does. This may mean designing a logo with no set
typeface, or an unlimited range of colors, or no logo at all.
On the whole, clients now seem to accept that there fewer
rules in logo and identity work.

**What is the most important job for a logo to do?**
To be noticed, engaging, and remembered.

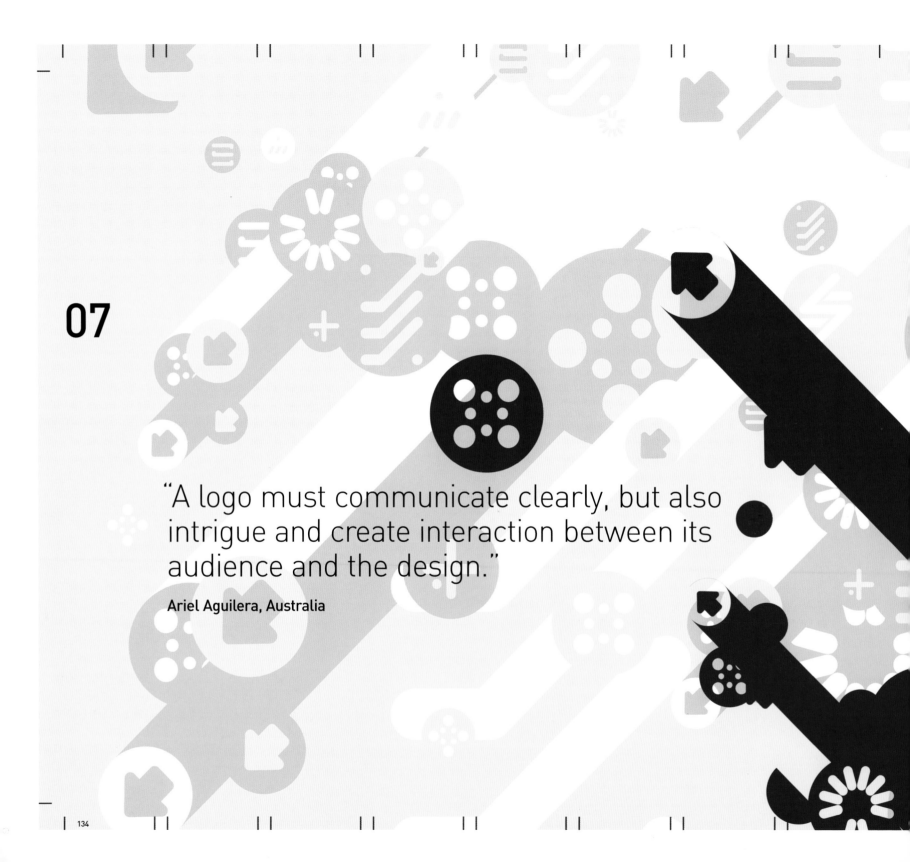

07

"A logo must communicate clearly, but also intrigue and create interaction between its audience and the design."

Ariel Aguilera, Australia

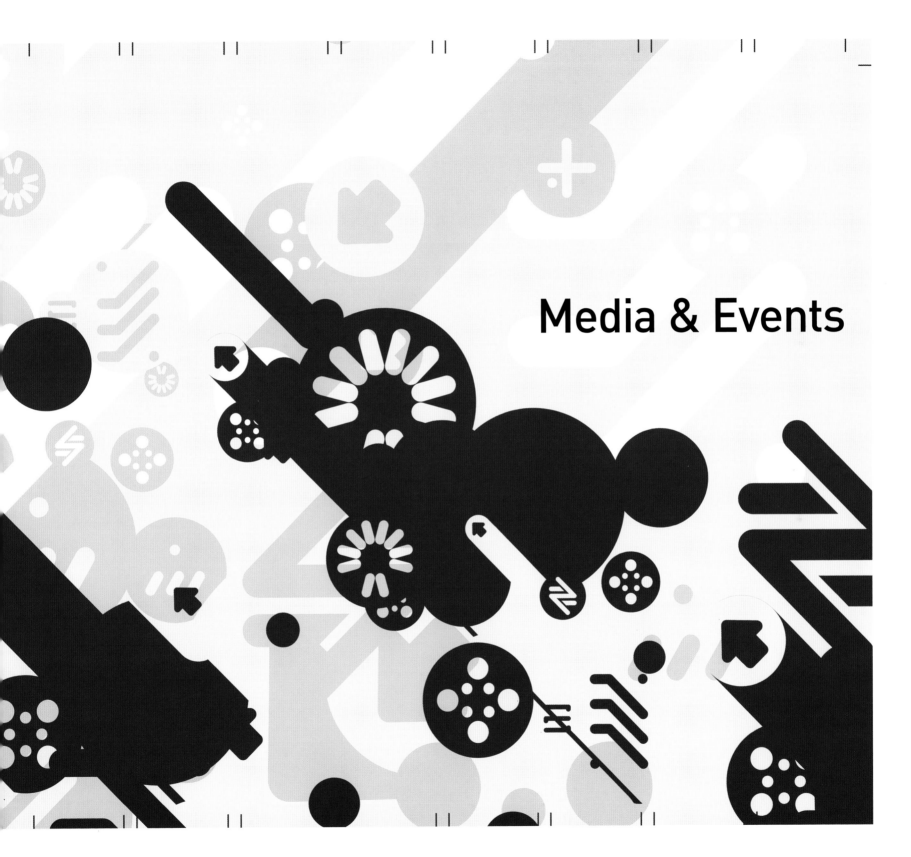

Media & Events

"The most successful logo is always
the next logo that we will create."

Jonas Hellström, Sweden

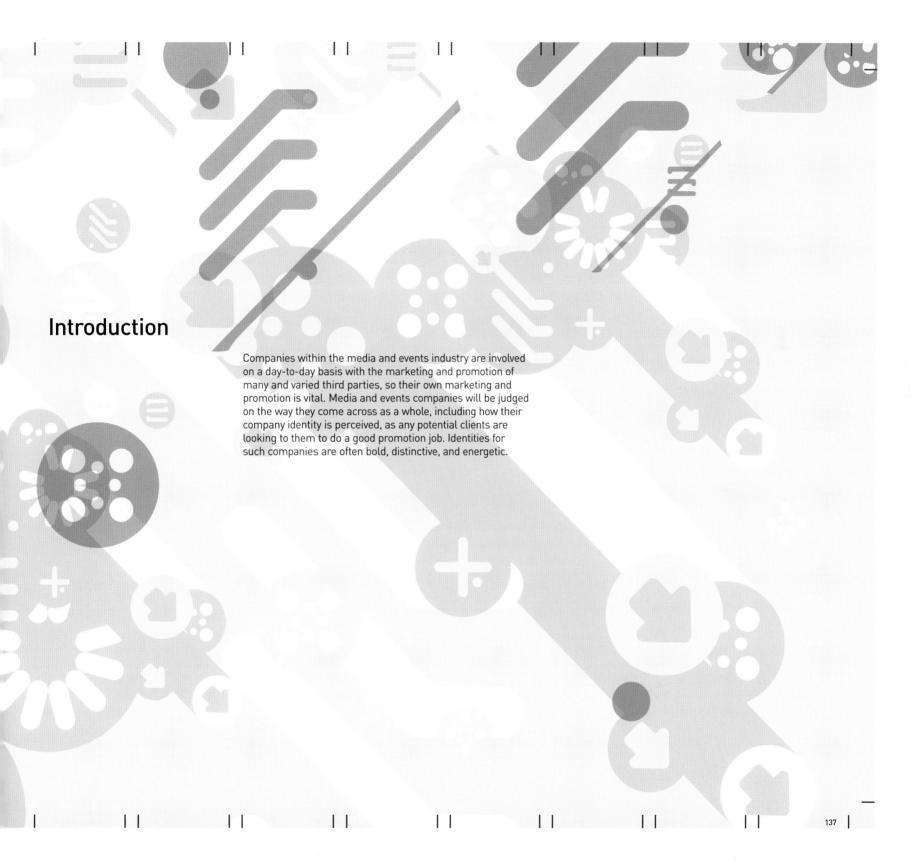

# Introduction

Companies within the media and events industry are involved on a day-to-day basis with the marketing and promotion of many and varied third parties, so their own marketing and promotion is vital. Media and events companies will be judged on the way they come across as a whole, including how their company identity is perceived, as any potential clients are looking to them to do a good promotion job. Identities for such companies are often bold, distinctive, and energetic.

Client: **Moth Design**
Design: **Pandarosa**
Country: **Australia**

## Adjust

Moth is a design collective consisting of multidisciplined designers (industrial, textile, and multimedia). It creates installations, furniture, events, and products, and also undertakes its own personal projects and workshops. Pandarosa created this logo for one of its installation/exhibition pieces, which it developed for the inaugural State of Design festival in Melbourne. The brief was to create an image related to the project's theme of human senses and the idea of "hyper senses." The logo's hand image was based on a palmistry symbol, which indicates various zones and their meanings within the palm. By combining this symbol with imagery of trees and roots, Pandarosa wanted to create an organic living image that expressed the sensory nature of the project, and also represented the "hand" as a vehicle for interaction between the project and its viewers. The logo featured on the exhibition catalog, invitations, posters, and signage.

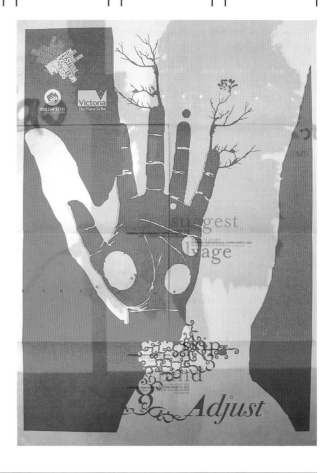

Client: **Will Wilson/Dave Goodbourn**
Design: **Mat Fowler at Playarea**
Country: **UK**

## Laboratory Media

Laboratory Media is a digital media company specializing in DVD production and audiovisual exhibition. It asked Playarea to create an identity to reflect professionalism, clarity, and conciseness. Continuing the laboratory theme set up by the company name, the identity is based around the iconic visual palette of the periodic table. "We styled the company initials as a direct play on the 'elements' of the periodic table," explains Fowler. "This idea was then used across various applications including business cards, on which the company director's initials were twinned with the company name." Akzidenz Grotesk was chosen for its clear, concise, and utilitarian qualities. The logo has been applied to a range of stationery items, and on mugs for the company owners.

Client: **Chris Bilheimer**
Design: **Chris Bilheimer**
Country: **USA**

## Chris Bilheimer

Bilheimer developed this logo to promote a talk he gave at the AIGA. "This was a completely new logo for my existing personal design work," he explains. "I'd never really had a set logo for myself before, so this was a fun opportunity to come up with something. I had no specific requirements for it, other than I wanted it to make me laugh. It means something to me on a couple of levels: one, it is funny, and two, it comes from a story from my childhood—I thought it would be funny to teach my dogs to walk each other." Bilheimer drew the images of the dogs based on existing reference photographs and used Futura typeface in the logo.

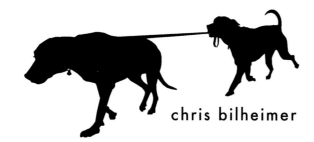

Client: **BrandIgloo**
Design: **Daniel Goddemeyer**
Country: **Germany**

## BrandIgloo

Goddemeyer, who founded BrandIgloo, created this logo for its launch. "The idea was very straightforward," he explains. "We wanted to make use of the imagery of an igloo, since the name BrandIgloo had a very concrete association with this." The logo features an illustration of an igloo together with a logotype based on the typeface Leger.

Client: **Videotage**
Design: **Javin Mo at milkxhake**
Country: **Hong Kong**

## Let Art Disturb U

Let Art Disturb U is an experimental
project by milkxhake in collaboration
with Videotage, a media arts organization.
The project is intended to act as a platform
for promoting both international media
and new media arts archives to a local
audience. "The project title and logotype
were inspired by the traditional 'Do Not
Disturb' sign," explains Mo. "Bouncing
from country to country, biennial to
triennial, 'Let Art Disturb U' is the hotel
for everyone to check into: this is where
art sheds its elitism and returns to
everyday life." The logo's simple outline
is filled with a prominent red. The project
itself became an editorial feature in the
local weekly pop culture magazine.

© milkxhake 2006

Client: **BrandIgloo**
Design: **Daniel Goddemeyer**
Country: **Germany**

## SecretDiary

SecretDiary is an online diary for two set up by BrandIgloo (see page 139), and its first product launch. As this logo was designed for a website sold in real packaging, its main requirement was to work both on- and offline. "The idea of the SecretDiary—two people, separated by distance, but still feeling close to each other in the online diary—is depicted by the two butterflies in the logo," explains Goddemeyer. The hand-drawn butterflies are accompanied by a logotype that is based on the ITC Bauhaus font. The logo has been applied to SecretDiary packaging, website, posters, and postcards.

Client: **Flaunt**
Design: **Rilla Alexander at Rinzen**
Country: **Germany**

## Flaunt

Rinzen designed the logo for the launch of Flaunt, a marketing and communications company. The brief was to create a bold, individual, and distinctive identity. "We wanted the logo to feel somewhat energetic and playful so that it reflected both the meaning behind the word 'flaunt' and the personality of the company itself," explains Alexander. Using a specially created typeface, the logotype was informed largely by the individual letterforms and their relationship to each other. It appears on the company's stationery and communication materials.

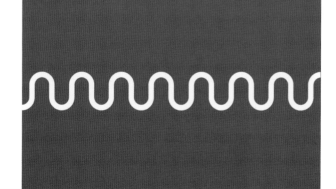

Barrie Barton
Director
M 0416 153 019
barrie@flaunt.net.au

**Flaunt**
607/166 Flinders Street Melbourne VIC 3000
PH +61 3 9662 2607
www.flaunt.net.au

Client: **Dimaquina**
Design: **Antônio Pedro/Daniel Neves/
     Alex Nako**
Countries: **Brazil/UK**

## Dimaquina

Dimaquina is a design collective that focuses on a multidisciplinary approach to design and believes in collaborative creativity between designers and client. Its logo had to signal the studio's passion for design as well as its informal and unpretentious way of looking at things. "The typographic approach reveals the design finesse the studio aims for, with knowledge and control over the design tools," explains Nako. "The logo is fairly subtle, and the symbol, which came at a later stage, proved to have extreme character and versatility because of its simple and cohesive form." The logo has been used on Dimaquina's website, stationery, and promotional materials.

# Dimaquina

Client: **red-hot**
Design: **Alexander Egger**
Country: **Austria**

## red-hot

red-hot is a small communications and marketing agency. It commissioned Egger to design a logo to reflect its core competencies: innovative marketing concepts and creativity. The resultant logo consists of the printed "r" with a red underline defining a blank space that is filled in by the respective contact at the agency. "The core values of the agency are demonstrated and practiced directly within the usage of the identity system," explains Egger. "Filling out the name of a particular staff member in front of the client before handing over a business card shows a transparent company and is a demonstration of the ability to come up with creative ideas." The logo has been used on its stationery and website.

# Eight ™

abcdEfghjjxcm
noPqrSturwxy2
123456789o

Client: **Eight**
Design: **Tom Lancaster at Stylo Design**
Country: **UK**

## Eight

Eight is an events management company with eight founding members. "The brief for the logo was very loose," explains Lancaster. "Essentially they were looking to us for ideas and creativity as well as execution so we picked up on the simple fact there were eight of them and went from there. We began experimenting with the '8' character and this led to the design of an experimental typeface, which in turn led to the solution—a logo derived entirely from the numeral 8." The logo has been applied across all corporate literature, stationery, and marketing materials, with foil blocking and blind embossing used on all printed materials.

Client: **desres design group**
Design: **Michaela Kessler and Dirk Schrod at desres design group**
Country: **Germany**

## desres is on

This self-promotional logo was created for the launch of the desres design group, a design and consultancy studio active in a wide range of projects across a growing variety of media, from concept design and illustration to interactive design and typography. The logo is based on the phrase "desres is on," and features a light installation as the key visual. The designers have used fifty ceiling lights to form an illuminated version of the word "on." Front and back shots of the visual have been used as the logo on company invitations, website, and postcards.

Client: **Isla Media**
Design: **Paul Sych at Faith**
Country: **Canada**

## Isla

Publishing company Isla Media commissioned Sych to design a logo for its launch. "The client had come up with the name 'Isla' while vacationing in Mexico," explains Sych. "They wanted me to consider the word association of 'island' in English in developing concepts for the logo." Sych's design was inspired by Aztec and Mexican culture as well as typography. The logo uses a decorative, custom-drawn typeface that has been applied to the company's stationery.

Client: **Superkronik Club**
Design: **Via Grafik**
Country: **Germany**

### Kill Boredom

Superkronik is a small nightclub and gallery that combines club nights with exhibitions. As part of an exhibition, Via Grafik was invited to paint the walls of the club. The theme of the exhibition was "Kill Boredom." Via Grafik was also asked to create a logo for the show. For this it designed a custom-made typeface, and "borrowed" the black-and-yellow color combination used on walls throughout the club. The logo was applied on the mural, fliers, and posters created to promote the exhibition.

Client: **Via Grafik/Everwanting Streets**
Design: **André Nossek/Via Grafik**
Countries: **Germany/Sweden**

### Let's Be Chaotic

Everwanting Streets was a big street-art exhibition held in Gothenburg. Via Grafik was invited to take part and paint a mural on one of the gallery walls. "We painted a big collage, the main theme of which was 'let's be chaotic,' which is one of our collectives' mottos." They also designed a logo which was incorporated into the mural and onto buttons. The typeface was based on Helvetica, with some letter bowls being filled in to "destroy" them, carrying on the theme of the exhibition—chaos and unpredictability.

Client: **University of the Arts London/Imperial College London/ Wellcome Trust**
Design: **Christian Küsters at CHK Design**
Country: **UK**

## How Do You Look?

How Do You Look? is a traveling exhibition for which Küsters was asked to create a logo and identity. The exhibition logo directly reflects the eye-tracker biomedical tool, which was used in the exhibition's research as it records fixations, saccades, and gaze paths. The human gaze shifts from one point to the next (the fixations) with very rapid linear movements (the saccades). As most of the time we look with a purpose (to read, to search, to understand, to undertake a task, etc), our gaze path reflects what goes on in our minds, either consciously or subconsciously. This science of looking directly affected CHK's ideas for the exhibition's identity. The final logo design, which is constructed to function as a strong identity, visually displays how the viewer looks at it; the connecting red lines mirroring saccades and their consequent fixations and gaze paths. The logo typeface is AF Cashier. The logo was used for all facets of the exhibition. It was also produced in vinyl lettering to cover the front of the gallery.

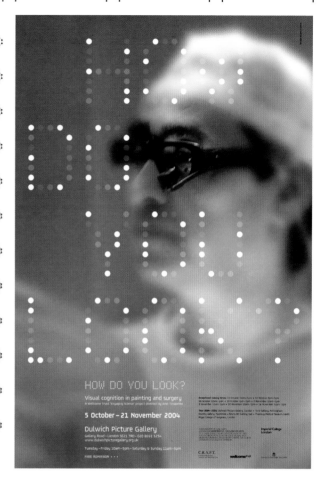

Client: **designforum**
Design: **Alexander Egger**
Country: **Austria**

## Re:cycle

Re:cycle, an exhibition about sustainable packaging design, was held at designforum, Vienna, in 2006. The logo consists of a two-color, double title in a stencil-style font—a modified VAG Rounded—chosen because of its origins in industry and production. A pattern was created by repeating the logo on wrapping paper, which was then wrapped around elements such as traffic signs and benches around the exhibition venue in order to promote the event. "The exhibition identity reflects maximum flexibility and openness for change and constructive contribution," explains Egger.

# RE: RE:CYCLE CYCLE

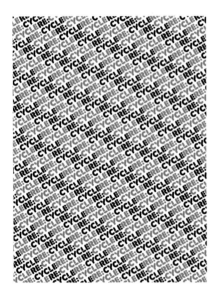

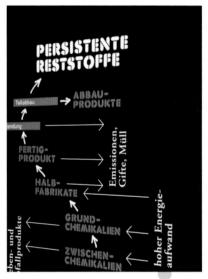

# ABCDEFGHIJKLMNOPQRSTUVWXYZ
# 1234567890

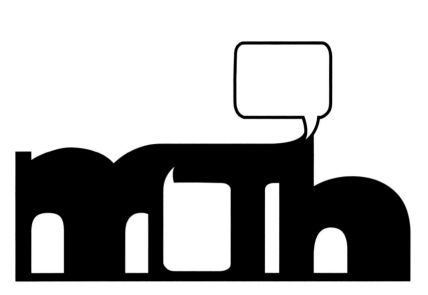

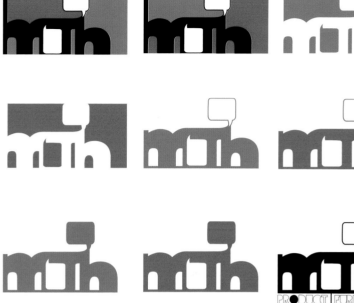

Client: **Moth Design**
Design: **Ariel Aguilera and Andrea Benyi**
     **at Pandarosa**
Country: **Australia**

## Moth Design

Moth is a design collective consisting of multidisciplined designers (industrial, textile, and multimedia). It creates installations, furniture, events, and products, and also undertakes its own personal projects and workshops. "The concept was to express the dialogue and interaction of the group by the simple use of speech bubbles," explain Aguilera and Benyi. "We wanted to keep this visual within the word 'Moth' to keep everything clear and precise." Pandarosa played with various options, using negative and positive forms, until they were happy with the result. By using one of the speech bubbles as an "O," it created a logo that is in constant dialogue with itself. The logo appears on the company's signage, stationery, and website.

Client: **Microsoft**
Design: **Nikolaj Knop at WE RECOMMEND**
Country: **Sweden**

## Loose Ends

WE RECOMMEND in collaboration with Futurelab, a strategy and communication agency, created this logo for a campaign run by software producer Microsoft. "When we were briefed, we were asked to create a logo that looked nothing like the kind of thing people were used to seeing from Microsoft," explains Knop. To this end, WE RECOMMEND has created an edgy, noncorporate logotype with a custom-designed font. In addition, each letter features different imagery shot by WE RECOMMEND. "We wanted to add texture and content to the logotype," explains Knop.

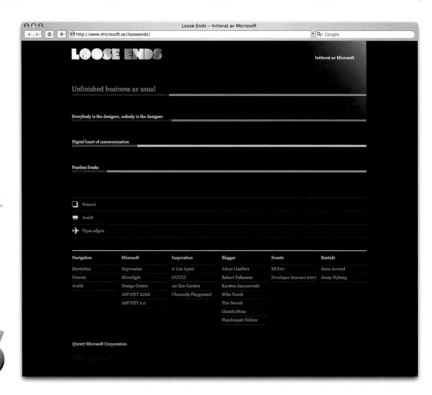

Client: **Kamel Mennour Gallery**
Design: **Yorgo Tloupas**
Country: **France**

## Kamel Mennour

Kamel Mennour launched his art gallery in 2001. Since then it has grown to become a player on the international art scene. The logo shown here was designed to mark the extension of the gallery into a new, larger space. "The client wanted an instantly recognizable sign to mark out the gallery in the sea of look-alike adverts in the art press," Tloupas explains. "It also wanted to establish itself as a more mature and serious gallery, with a strict global identity, and to remain sober and elegant." Tloupas decided to create a symbol that would be utterly basic and as close as possible to the primary geometric shapes. He also wanted a sign with second-degree readability, that is, not immediately readable. "By positioning these three triangles in such a way it created a 'countershape,' a white square, which is reminiscent of the quintessential gallery space," adds Tloupas. "The simplicity of the logo allows it to be used small-scale, as an accent or asterisk to the gallery name, and to be reproduced as a pattern." Tloupas created a specific font for the project, titled the Kamelle, which is based on the existing Eurofurence typeface.

Client: **LABS**
Design: **David Weik at Studio UKV**
Country: **USA**

## LABS

LABS is a small interactive design and marketing office, based in Chicago, which utilizes a worldwide network of designers and developers. Studio UKV created the LABS logo as part of its new identity and branding campaign. Its brief was to create a logo that was clean, simple, and modern, and suggested the intertwined, cellular nature of the company's global network. "I wanted the stationery to provide a classic, timeless environment for the logo to reside in; extending the half-life of the identity and giving the brand a bit of grace," explains Weik. "The pattern within the logo was included to provide a secondary element for the brand and to help reinforce the idea of network."

## Ariel Aguilera, Pandarosa, Australia

**What do you think makes a good logo?**
Clarity and variety. It's important to have a nongeneric approach toward logo design so one can aim to create something more personal or with a unique touch.

**Which are your favorite three logos?**
This is a really difficult question, as there are numerous memorable and important logos throughout history. So we have come up with three categories that include some of our favorites. Nostalgia: Transformers Autobot and Decepticon logos (1984 cartoon) and LEGO—we don't remember them so much as logos, but as images we grew up with. Chronicle: Public Enemy and Blue Note Records—identities that symbolize the times socially and musically. Simplicity: Atari and the peace symbol—timeless icons created using the simplest of approaches.

**What has been your most successfully designed logo?**
Probably the logo we designed for Platform Artists Group Inc. We were able to continuously "reinterpret" the logo, creating numerous applications (posters, signage, invites, etc.) without using the simple formula of repeating the logo over and over again. It was a refreshing way to create a logo without using repetition as the only vehicle for communication.

**When approaching the design of a logo what inspires you?**
We usually start by talking to the client about the philosophies and aims behind their business. We then start to research the title or name of the logo, looking for any interesting meanings or aspects of the title that can transcend from written into visual form.

**In some cases there are many places a logo may need to be applied—how much of a consideration is that when designing a logo?**
A big one is that it needs to transcend through all possible applications without losing any of its impact or communication.

**What is the most important job for a logo?**
To communicate clearly, but also to intrigue and create interaction between its audience and the design. People aren't as stupid as some businesses may like to think, and we don't believe that pushing your logo at people is the only way to make them recognize you or your image.

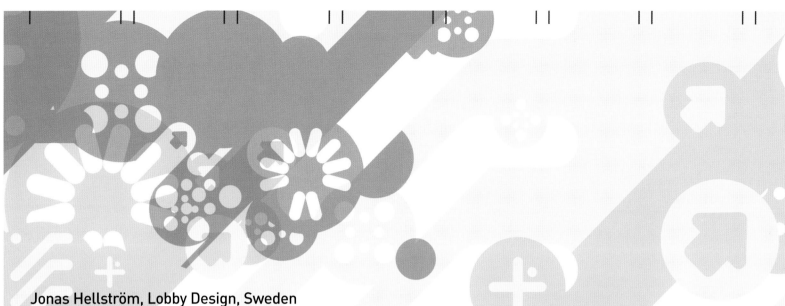

## Jonas Hellström, Lobby Design, Sweden

**What do you think makes a good logo?**
A good logo must have character. It should be clear, relative to the subject, and innovative enough to stick out. But the most important thing is that the logo be based on a good idea or concept. Color and shape are secondary. The look is important, but, without idea or content, it merely looks, and is uninteresting in the long run.

**Which are your favorite three logos?**
We mention four logos instead of three. The Sun Microsystems logo designed by Professor Vaughan Pratt because of its clever geometry. The Apple logo designed by Rob Janoff because of its simplicity and yet many levels. Is it the apple that the snake gave to Eve? Is it the apple that whacked Newton on the head? Taking a bite should mean knowledge either way. The Nike logo designed by intern Carolyn Davidson because of its simplicity. It has a good story and it's probably the world's best-recognized commercial pictogram. The Mont Blanc logo, designer unknown to us, because of its brilliant idea and simplicity.

**What has been your most successfully designed logo?**
The most successful logo is always the next logo that we will create!

**When approaching the design of a logo what inspires you?**
We always get inspiration from within the company and start with research relative to the subject. If we're to design a logo for a spaceship, we delve into space rather than books and magazines. We start as far back as possible. The more information you get the better. This is not true every time though. Sometimes the opposite is a good start.

**In some cases there are many places a logo may need to be applied—how much of a consideration is that when designing a logo?**
It should be of consideration in the first steps of designing a logo. You will always have to think bigger when designing a logo because the logo will not only be printed on a business card. You must think big and small, otherwise the logo is not the perfect logo. A logo should always work anywhere in any format.

**What is the most important job for a logo?**
To express the soul of the company/brand. It should stand for the same values as the company/brand or the values of the company's preferred customer. And, of course, to make people remember you.

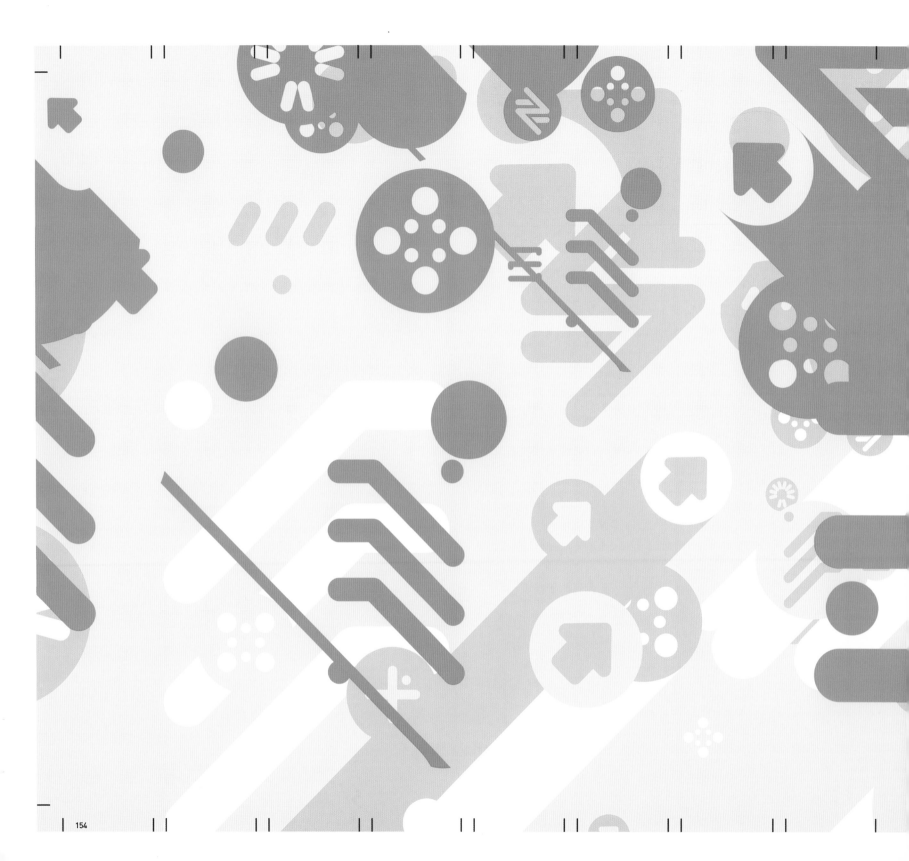

# Contact Details & Acknowledgments

# Contact Details

310k
www.310k.nl / we@310k.nl

3 Deep Design
www.3deep.com.au / design@3deep.com.au

Christian Albriktsen
albriks@gmail.com

Elisabeth Arkhipoff
www.romanticsurf.com / elisabeth@romanticsurf.com

Tatiana Arocha
www.tatianaarocha.com / tatiana@servicio-ejecutivo.com

A-Side Studio
www.a-sidestudio.co.uk / contact@a-sidestudio.co.uk

Atelier Michel Bouvet
atelierbouvet@wanadoo.fr

BankerWessel
www.bankerwessel.com / info@bankerwessel.com

Base Design
www.basedesign.com / basenyc@basedesign.com

BB/Saunders
www.bbsaunders.com / martin@bbsaunders.com

Chris Bilheimer
www.bilheimer.com / crb@chronictown.com

Birdseed
www.youneedbirdseed.com / birdseed@artserve.net

Braveland Design
www.bravelanddesign.com / braveland@earthlink.net

Browns
www.brownsdesign.com / jonathan@brownsdesign.com

Stefan G. Bucher for 344 Design, LLC
344design.com / stefan.bucher@344design.com

C100 Studio
www.c100studio.com / hello@c100studio.com

Caótica
www.caotica.com.br / caotica@caotica.com.br

Chemical Box
www.chemicalbox.com / bureau@chemicalbox.com

CHK Design
www.chkdesign.com / info@chkdesign.com

Ryan Clark
invisiblecreature.com / ryan@invisiblecreature.com

Stefan Claudius
www.claudius-design.de / stefan@claudius-design.de

Codeluxe
codeluxe.com / buero@codeluxe.com

Deanne Cheuk
www.deannecheuk.com / neomuworld@aol.com

Designbolaget
www.designbolaget.dk / due@designbolaget.dk

Design People Studio
www.designpeople.net / talk@designpeople.net

Desorg
www.desorg.cl / flavio@desorg.cl

desres design group
www.desres.de / contact@desres.de

Dimaquina
www.dimaquina.com / info@dimaquina.com

Alexander Egger
www.satellitesmistakenforstars.com /
alex@satellitesmistakenforstars.com

Emmi
www.emmi.co.uk / hello@emmi.co.uk

Engine Creative
www.enginecreative.co.uk / hello@enginecreative.co.uk

env design
www.env-design.com / we@env-design.com

Matthias Ernstberger
studio@matthiasernstberger.com

Faith (Paul Sych)
www.faith.ca / paul@faith.ca

General Working Group
www.generalworkinggroup.com / geoff@generalworkinggroup.com

Daniel Goddemeyer
www.someprojects.org / daniel@someprojects.org

Grafikonstruct
www.grafikonstruct.com.br / info@grafikonstruct.com.br

GraphicTherapy
www.graphictherapy.com / david@graphictherapy.com

Honey Design
www.honeydesign.com / rina@honeydesign.com

Hudson-Powell
www.hudson-powell.com / luke@hudson-powell.com

Hyperkit
www.hyperkit.co.uk / info@hyperkit.co.uk

Invisible Creature
invisiblecreature.com / ryan@invisiblecreature.com

karlssonwilker inc.
www.karlssonwilker.com / tellmewhy@karlssonwilker.com

Lobby Design
www.lobbydesign.se / info@lobbydesign.se

Michael Mandrup
www.40606005.dk / info@40606005.dk

Luca Marchettoni (Blumagenta Studio)
www.blumagenta.com / luca@w3d.it

milkxhake
www.milkxhake.org / mix@milkxhake.org

Mono (Julio Dui)
www.mono.com.br / dui@mono.com.br

Andy Mueller
www.ohiogirl.com / andy@ohiogirl.com

Neighbour
phil@neighbour-uk.com / www.neighbour-uk.com

No Days Off
www.nodaysoff.com / info@nodaysoff.com

ODD
www.thankodd.com / info@thankodd.com

Ohio Girl
andy@ohiogirl.com / www.ohiogirl.com

Ollystudio
www.ollystudio.co.uk / info@ollystudio.co.uk

One-two.org
www.one-two.org / r.muntwyler@one-two.org

Pandarosa
www.pandarosa.net / info@pandarosa.net

Park Studio
www.park-studio.com / park@park-studio.com

Peter and Paul
www.peterandpaul.co.uk / paul@peterandpaul.co.uk

Playarea
www.play-area.co.uk / info@play-area.co.uk

PMKFA
www.pmkfa.com / micke@pmkfa.com

Adam Pointer
www.adampointer.com / adampointer@yahoo.co.uk

Proud Creative
www.proudcreative.com / hello@proudcreative.com

Purple Haze Studio
www.thepurplehaze.net / hello@thepurplehaze.net

Ranch
www.ranchdesign.co.uk / info@ranchdesign.co.uk

Rinzen
www.rinzen.com / they@rinzen.com

Roanne Adams Design
www.roanneadams.com / ro@roanneadams.com

Richard Robinson
www.richardrobinsondesign.co.uk /
richardrobinson@blueyonder.co.uk

Ryan Meis
www.ryanmeis.com / ryan@ryanmeis.com

Sagmeister Inc.
www.sagmeister.com / info@sagmeister.com

Studio Dumbar
www.studiodumbar.com / info@studiodumbar.com

Studio Oscar
www.wilsonbrothers.co.uk / www.benwilsondesign.co.uk
www.studiooscar.com / info@studiooscar.com

Studio UKV
www.studioukv.com / info@studioukv.com

Stylo Design
www.stylodesign.co.uk / info@stylodesign.co.uk

This Studio
www.this-studio.co.uk / david@this-studio.co.uk

Tilt Design Studio
www.tiltdesignstudio.com / info@tiltdesignstudio.com

Yorgo Tloupas
www.yorgo.co.uk / yorgo@yorgo.co.uk

Underline Studio (Clea Forkert)
www.underlinestudio.com / fidel@underlinestudio.com

Undoboy
www.undoboy.com / contact@undoboy.com

Via Grafik
www.vgrfk.com / leo@vgrfk.com

Oliver Walker
www.ollystudio.co.uk / olly@ollystudio.co.uk

WE RECOMMEND
www.werecommend.se / mail@werecommend.se

Ellen Zhao
www.buro-gds.com / ellen.gds@gmail.com

Zion Graphics
www.ziongraphics.com / ricky@ziongraphics.com

# Acknowledgments

Many thanks to all the designers around the world who submitted work for inclusion in Logo-Art. Special thanks to Emmi Salonen, Adrian Clifford, Olly Walker, Rina Miele, Ross Imms, Stefan Sagmeister, Ben Cave, Andy Mueller, Christian Küsters, Paul Reardon, Ariel Aguilera, and Jonas Hellström.

Once again thank-you to the team at RotoVision, and to Simon Slater for his great design job.

This book is for Mum.

# Index